Fun Systematic Theology for Kids

52 Week Adventure to Understand Who God Is, Explore Bible Truth, Learn Core Beliefs, Grow Strong Habits, and Make Faith Real Each Day

Wonder & Word Press

First edition 2026

Contents

Introduction

You are about to do something most adults have never done.

Over the next 52 weeks, you are going to study God. Not just learn a few Bible verses or memorize some Sunday school answers. You are going to ask the biggest questions anyone can ask: Who is God, really? What is He like? Why does any of this matter? And you are going to follow those questions all the way down to solid ground.

That is what theology is. It is the study of God. And it is the greatest adventure a person can go on.

Here is what is waiting for you inside this book.

Every week begins with a story about a kid your age wrestling with a real question about God. From there, you will dig into what the Bible actually says, explore the scriptures that speak to it, and land on a verse to carry with you all week. You will find activities to help you think things through for yourself. There are questions to check what you have learned. And at the end of every week, a challenge waits for you to take what you studied out into the world and actually live it.

There are 52 weeks organized into 12 units, each one building on the one before it. You can work through it on your own, with a parent, or with a class. One week at a time is all it takes.

Two helpful resources are waiting for you at the back of this book. First, the **Answer Key**, which includes every answer for all 52 weeks so you can check your work. Second, the **Theology Dictionary**, which contains every theology word introduced throughout the book, along with a pronunciation guide and a full definition for each one. Both the Answer Key and the Theology Dictionary are **downloadable**. Simply scan the QR codes at the back of the book to download your free copies. You do not need to already know a lot about God to start this book. You just need to be curious. And if you are holding this, you probably already are.

So. Are you ready?

Let's go find out who God actually is.

One

Knowing God

Weeks 1 through 7

Who is God? What is He like? And why does knowing Him matter? Seven weeks on the foundations of knowing God.

Weeks in this unit:

- Week 1: What Is Theology, and Why Does It Matter?
- Week 2: How Do We Know God Is Real?
- Week 3: God Never Changes
- Week 4: God Is Everywhere, Knows Everything, Can Do Anything
- Week 5: God Is Holy
- Week 6: God Is Love, and God Is Just
- Week 7: Unit 1 Review

Week 1: What Is Theology, and Why Does It Matter?

What does it mean to study God, and why should I bother?

Zoe was nine years old and had a lot of questions.

At school, she asked questions about science and math. At home, she asked questions about why things worked the way they did. And lately, she had been asking questions about God.

One Sunday, her teacher said a word Zoe had never heard before.

'Theology,' her teacher said.

'What is that?' Zoe asked.

'It is the study of God. It means asking questions about who God is, what He is like, and what He has done.'

Zoe liked that idea. She already had a whole list of God questions stored up inside her head. Questions about why the world was broken, about whether God actually heard prayers, about what happened after people died.

'So asking questions about God is a good thing?' she said.

'One of the best things you can do,' her teacher said. 'Questions are how we grow. And God is big enough to handle every one of yours.'

Zoe pulled out her notebook and started writing them down.

Theology Is Just a Big Word for Knowing God

The word theology comes from two Greek words. Theos means God. Logos means word or study. Together they mean the study of God.

You might think theology is only for grown-ups or people who have been to college. But that is not true. Every person who asks questions about God is already doing theology. You have probably been doing it for years without knowing what to call it.

Jesus said the most important thing anyone can do is love God with their whole heart, soul, mind, and strength. (Mark 12:30.) Loving God well begins with knowing Him well. Theology is how we get to know Him.

Asking Questions Is a Good Thing

Some people worry that asking hard questions about God means they do not have enough faith. But the Bible disagrees.

Proverbs 2:4-5 says that if we search for wisdom like hidden treasure, we will find the knowledge of God. Searching requires questions. You cannot find hidden treasure without looking for it.

The disciples asked Jesus questions constantly. The Psalms are full of honest questions directed straight at God. Asking is not doubt. It is how we grow.

Why It Matters

Knowing who God actually is changes everything about how we live.

If we think of God as an angry rule-keeper, we will be afraid of Him. If we think of Him as a distant force, we will not bother with Him. If we know Him as He actually is, a personal, loving, powerful God who is completely trustworthy, everything changes.

Theology is not just information. It is the beginning of a relationship with the most important person in the universe.

Key Verses

"Love the Lord your God with all your heart and with all your soul and with all your mind and with all your strength." (Mark 12:30)

"If you look for it as for silver and search for it as for hidden treasure, then you will find the knowledge of God."

(Proverbs 2:4-5)

This Week's Verse to Memorize

Proverbs 2:4-5

"If you look for it as for silver and search for it as for hidden treasure, then you will find the knowledge of God."

The search is worth it. Write this verse out and then write one question about God you genuinely want to find the answer to this year.

Activities

Activity 1: My God Questions

Write down five genuine questions you have about God. Do not worry if they feel too big or too hard. Write the ones you actually have. Keep this list. By the end of this workbook, come back and see which ones you can answer.

Activity 2: Theology in One Sentence

Without using a dictionary, write a definition of theology in your own words. Keep it under two sentences. Then write one reason why you personally think knowing God matters.

Quiz Time

Answer these questions in your journal or workbook:

1. What does the word theology mean?

2. Where does the word theology come from?

3. According to Mark 12:30, what is the most important thing we can do?

4. What does Proverbs 2:4-5 say we should search for?

5. Why does it matter what we believe about who God is?

This Week's Challenge

This week, ask one adult in your life what they think is the most important thing to know about God. Write down what they say. You do not need to agree. Just listen and record it.

New Words to Know

Theology: The study of God. From the Greek words theos (God) and logos (word or study).

Disciple: A follower and learner. All Christians are disciples, which means they are always learning.

Attribute: A quality or characteristic. When we talk about God's attributes, we mean the qualities that describe who He is.

Week 2: How Do We Know God Is Real?

Is there actual evidence that God exists?

Marco's friend at school told him that God was just something people made up to feel better.

Marco had not known how to answer that. The words had stuck with him for days.

He finally brought the question to his grandfather one evening.

'How do we actually know God is real?' Marco asked. 'Not just that we believe He is. That He actually exists.'

His grandfather was quiet for a moment. Then he pointed out the window at the sky.

'Where did all of that come from?' he asked.

'The universe?' Marco said. 'Scientists say the Big Bang.'

'Right. And what caused the Big Bang?'

Marco thought about it. 'I do not know.'

'Neither does anyone else,' his grandfather said. 'Every explanation eventually runs into the same wall. Something had to start it. And whatever started everything had to be outside of everything, more powerful than everything, and not itself caused by anything. That description fits God very well.'

'Is that proof?' Marco asked.

'It is a very good reason,' his grandfather said. 'And there is more where that came from.'

The Universe Had to Come from Somewhere

Everything that exists had a beginning. Scientists agree the universe began at a specific point. But what caused it?

Whatever caused the universe has to be outside of time and space, incredibly powerful, and not itself caused by something else. That description fits God perfectly.

Romans 1:20 says God's invisible qualities have been clearly seen through what He has made, so that people are without excuse.

The World Shows Signs of Design

A watch implies a watchmaker. A painting implies a painter. The universe is vastly more complex than either.

The human eye alone contains over a hundred million light-sensitive cells working together. DNA stores more information than the most advanced computers ever built. The conditions needed for life on Earth are so precise that scientists call it the fine-tuning problem.

Design implies a designer. Psalm 19:1 says the heavens declare the glory of God. Creation is not silent. It is speaking.

God Has Revealed Himself

Beyond creation, God has spoken directly. He has revealed Himself through the Bible, through history, and most completely through Jesus.

John 1:18 says no one has ever seen God, but Jesus has made Him known. Jesus did not just talk about God. He showed us what God is like by how He lived, what He said, and what He was willing to do for us.

The clearest evidence for God is not found in a telescope. It is found in a person.

Key Verses

"The heavens declare the glory of God; the skies proclaim the work of his hands." (Psalm 19:1)

"For since the creation of the world God's invisible qualities...have been clearly seen, being understood from what has been made." (Romans 1:20)

This Week's Verse to Memorize

Psalm 19:1

"The heavens declare the glory of God; the skies proclaim the work of his hands."

Creation has been speaking about God since the beginning. Write this verse and then go outside and look at the sky. Write one sentence about what it makes you think about God.

Activities

Activity 1: Evidence Collector

Look around you this week for three things in creation that seem too complex or beautiful to be accidental. Write each one down and explain in one sentence what it suggests about the God who made it.

Activity 2: Questions and Answers

Write down the best argument you have heard for God not being real. Then write the best response to it that you can. You do not need to fully resolve it. Just practice thinking it through honestly.

Quiz Time

Answer these questions in your journal or workbook:

1. According to Romans 1:20, what can be understood from looking at creation?

2. What does the complexity of the universe suggest about its origin?

3. What does Psalm 19:1 say the heavens do?

4. According to John 1:18, who has made God known?

5. What are two reasons someone might believe God is real?

This Week's Challenge

This week, go outside at night and look at the sky for five minutes without your phone. Just look. Then write two sentences about what you noticed and what it made you think about.

New Words to Know

Existence: Being real. When we talk about God's existence, we mean whether He is actually real and not just an idea.

Evidence: Reasons to believe something is true. Evidence does not always mean scientific proof. It includes signs that point toward a conclusion.

Revelation: God making Himself known. He reveals Himself through creation, through Scripture, and most fully through Jesus.

Week 3: God Never Changes

If God never changes, what does that mean for me?

Priya's grandmother had been sick for a long time.

One afternoon while they sat together in the quiet of her room, Priya asked the question she had been holding onto for weeks.

'Does God ever change his mind about loving us? Like, what if we mess up really badly? Does he stop?'

Her grandmother looked at her steadily for a moment.

'No,' she said. 'That is one of the most important things I have learned in a long life. God does not change. His love does not go up or down based on what I do. I have had long seasons where I walked away from him. I made choices I am not proud of. He did not walk away from me.'

'How do you know He did not?' Priya asked.

'Because he says so,' her grandmother said simply. 'And I have spent a long time watching him keep His word. I have never found him to be a liar.'

Priya thought about that. There was something very solid about it. Like something you could actually stand on.

God Does Not Change

The word for this is immutability. It means God is always and completely the same. He does not grow stronger or weaker. He does not improve or decline. He does not have good days and bad days.

Malachi 3:6 says: I the Lord do not change. James 1:17 says He is the Father of heavenly lights, with whom there is no variation or shadow due to change.

This is not a small fact. It is one of the most stabilizing truths in all of Scripture.

Why This Matters for You

Think about the most trustworthy person you know. Part of what makes them trustworthy is consistency. You know what to expect from them. They are the same person whether anyone is watching or not.

God is perfectly consistent in a way no human being is. Every promise He has ever made He will keep. Every truth He has ever spoken stays true. His love toward you today is exactly the same as it was before you were born, and it will be exactly the same on the worst day of your life.

Numbers 23:19 says God is not a human that He should lie, or a son of man that He should change His mind.

What Does Not Change About God

His character does not change. He is always holy, always loving, always just, always patient.

His Word does not change. Isaiah 40:8 says the word of our God endures forever.

His love does not change. Nothing you do can make God love you more than He already does. Nothing you do can make Him love you less. That love is not a feeling that fluctuates. It is a settled, permanent commitment.

Key Verses

"I the Lord do not change." (Malachi 3:6)

"Every good and perfect gift is from above, coming down from the Father of the heavenly lights, who does not change like shifting shadows." (James 1:17)

This Week's Verse to Memorize

Malachi 3:6

"I the Lord do not change."

Four words. The most stable promise in the universe. Write this verse and then write one area of your life where you need to remember that God does not change.

Activities

Activity 1: Change vs No Change

Write down five things in your life that change frequently: friendships, feelings, circumstances, opinions, weather. Then write one sentence about why it matters that God is not on that list.

Activity 2: Promise Tracker

Find three promises God makes in the Bible. Write each one down. Then write one sentence about why each promise is only trustworthy if God never changes.

Quiz Time

Answer these questions in your journal or workbook:

1. What is the word for God never changing?

2. What does Malachi 3:6 say about God?

3. According to Numbers 23:19, why can God be trusted to keep His promises?

4. Name three things about God that do not change.

5. Why is it comforting that God's love for you does not change based on what you do?

This Week's Challenge

Write down one promise from the Bible that you are trusting God to keep. Put it somewhere you will see it every day this week. Each morning, read it and remind yourself: the God who made this promise does not change.

New Words to Know

Immutability: The attribute of God meaning He never changes. From the Latin word mutare, meaning to change.

Promise: A commitment that something will happen. God's promises are trustworthy because His character never changes.

Faithful: Consistently keeping commitments over time. God is perfectly faithful because He is perfectly unchanging.

Week 4: God Is Everywhere, Knows Everything, Can Do Anything

What do the big words about God actually mean for my life?

Daniel had been sitting with a question for three days before he finally asked it.

'If God knows everything,' he said to his dad one evening, 'does that mean He already knew every bad thing I was going to do, even before I did it?'

'Yes,' his dad said simply.

Daniel was quiet for a long moment. 'And He still decided to love me? Knowing all of it?'

'He still decided to love you,' his dad said. 'He knew everything about you before you took your first breath. Every mistake, every selfish choice, every moment you would turn away from Him. He saw all of it. And He chose you anyway.'

Daniel looked out the window. 'I thought that would feel scary. But it does not.'

'No,' his dad said. 'Once it settles in, it is one of the most comforting things in the world. You are completely known and completely loved at the same time. Most people never experience that from another person. With God, it is just true.'

Omniscient: God Knows Everything

Omniscient means all-knowing. God knows every thought, every event, every moment of the past, present, and future. Nothing surprises Him. Nothing is hidden from Him.

Psalm 139:1-4 says God knows when we sit and when we rise. He perceives our thoughts from far away. He knows what we are going to say before the words leave our mouths.

This is not meant to feel threatening. It is meant to feel like finally being fully known and fully loved at the same time.

Omnipresent: God Is Everywhere

Omnipresent means God is fully present everywhere at once. There is no location in the universe where He is absent.

Psalm 139:7-10 says even if we go to the highest heaven or make our bed in the deepest depths, He is there. Even the darkness is not dark to Him.

You are never in a situation God that cannot see. You are never somewhere He cannot reach you. You are never truly alone.

Omnipotent: God Can Do Anything

Omnipotent means all-powerful. Nothing is beyond His ability. No problem is too large, no situation too far gone.

Jeremiah 32:17 says: Nothing is too hard for you. Genesis 18:14 asks: Is anything too hard for the Lord?

God does set one limit on Himself. He will not act against His own character. He cannot lie, and He cannot do evil. His power is always exercised in ways consistent with who He is. That is not a weakness. It is a guarantee.

Key Verses

"You have searched me, Lord, and you know me. You know when I sit and when I rise; you perceive my thoughts from afar." (Psalm 139:1-2)

"Nothing is too hard for you." (Jeremiah 32:17)

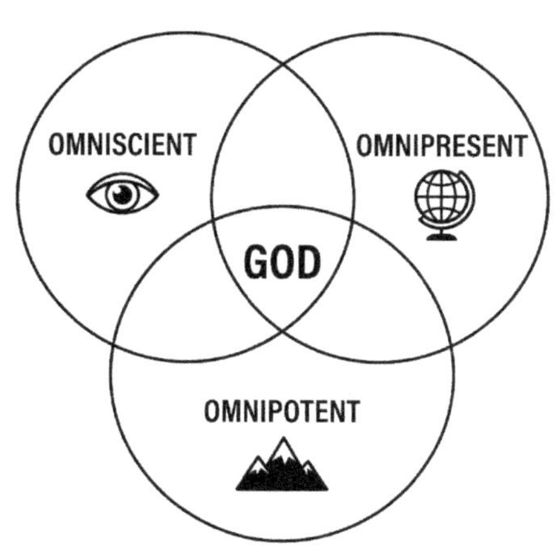

GOD DOES NOT CHANGE.
HE IS THE ANCHOR.

This Week's Verse to Memorize

Psalm 139:1-2

"You have searched me, Lord, and you know me. You know when I sit and when I rise; you perceive my thoughts from afar."

Being fully known and still fully loved is one of the greatest gifts in the Christian faith. Write this verse and then write one sentence about how it makes you feel to know that God knows you completely.

Activities

Activity 1: Three Words Three Meanings

Without looking at your notes, write a one-sentence definition of each of the three omni words. Then for each one, write one sentence about what it means for your daily life.

Activity 2: Psalm 139 Read-Through

Read all of Psalm 139. Write down three things David says God knows about him. Then write one sentence about whether that knowledge feels comforting or uncomfortable to you and why.

Quiz Time

Answer these questions in your journal or workbook:

1. What does omniscient mean?

2. What does omnipresent mean?

3. What does omnipotent mean?

4. According to Psalm 139:7-10, is there anywhere we can go where God is not present?

5. What is the one limit God places on His own power?

This Week's Challenge

This week, when you face something that feels too big or too hard, say out loud: God is here, God knows, and nothing is too hard for Him. Write at the end of the week about one situation where you tried this.

New Words to Know

Omniscient: All-knowing. God knows everything past, present, and future.

Omnipresent: Present everywhere at once. There is no place where God is absent.

Omnipotent: All-powerful. Nothing is beyond God's ability.

Omni: A Latin prefix meaning all or every. Used in all three words to describe God's unlimited nature.

Week 5: God Is Holy

What does holy mean, and why does it matter so much?

Sophie had been sitting in church when she heard something that bothered her for days.

Someone had said that God is so holy He cannot even look at sin.

She brought it to her mom that night.

'If God cannot look at sin, does that mean He looks away from me when I do something wrong?'

Her mom was quiet for a moment, choosing her words carefully.

'God is perfectly holy,' she said. 'And sin is a real and serious problem. But I do not think He looks away. I think the whole story of the Bible is the opposite of that. He looks directly at the mess we are in. He loves us so much that He refused to pretend it was not there. And He sent Jesus to fix it. His holiness is exactly why the cross was necessary. And His love is why He went through with it.'

Sophie thought about that. 'So holiness and love are not opposites?'

'In God, they never are,' her mom said.

What Holy Means

Holy means set apart and morally perfect. When we say God is holy, we mean He is completely unlike anything in creation. He is entirely pure, without any darkness, sin, or flaw of any kind.

Isaiah 6:3 records the seraphim around God's throne crying out: Holy, holy, holy is the Lord Almighty. In Hebrew, repeating a word three times was the way of expressing the absolute highest degree. God is not just holy. He is holy beyond any other thing we could call holy.

Holiness and Us

Because God is holy, sin is a serious problem. It is not a minor inconvenience or a misunderstanding. Romans 3:23 says all have sinned and fall short of the glory of God.

This is not meant to crush us. It is meant to help us understand exactly why we need rescue. A perfectly holy God and sinful people cannot simply pretend everything is fine. Something real has to be done about the gap between them.

That something is the gospel, which we will explore fully in Unit 6.

Holy Does Not Mean Distant

It would be easy to assume that because God is so holy, He keeps His distance from broken and sinful people. But the life of Jesus tells a completely different story.

Jesus ate meals with people everyone else avoided. He touched lepers. He spoke with people who had made terrible choices. His holiness did not shatter when it made contact with brokenness. Instead it healed and transformed.

First Peter 1:15-16 says: Be holy, because I am holy. The goal is not distance from God. It is becoming more like Him.

Key Verses

"Holy, holy, holy is the Lord Almighty; the whole earth is full of his glory." (Isaiah 6:3)

"For all have sinned and fall short of the glory of God." (Romans 3:23)

This Week's Verse to Memorize

Isaiah 6:3

"Holy, holy, holy is the Lord Almighty; the whole earth is full of his glory."

The angels never stop saying this. Write it out and then write one sentence about what it means for something to be holy to the highest possible degree.

Activities

Activity 1: What Holy Means

Write down three things described as holy in everyday life, such as holy ground or a holy day. For each one, explain what makes it holy. Then write one sentence about how God's holiness is different from all of them.

Activity 2: The Problem and the Solution

In your journal, write out the problem that God's holiness creates for sinful people. Then write one sentence about what you think the solution might be. We will come back to this in Unit 6.

Quiz Time

Answer these questions in your journal or workbook:

1. What does the word holy mean?

2. Why do the seraphim in Isaiah 6:3 say holy three times?

3. According to Romans 3:23, what is the human problem in relation to God's holiness?

4. Did Jesus stay away from sinful people? What does that tell us?

5. What does 1 Peter 1:15-16 call us to?

This Week's Challenge

This week, ask God to show you one specific area of your life where He is calling you to be more holy. Write it down. Do not try to fix it all at once. Just notice it and bring it to Him.

New Words to Know

Holy: Set apart and morally perfect. In relation to God, it means He is completely pure and unlike anything in creation.

Seraphim: Heavenly beings described in Isaiah 6 who surround God's throne and cry out about His holiness.

Sanctification: The process of becoming more holy. The Holy Spirit does this work in believers over time.

Sin: Anything that falls short of God's perfect standard. Romans 3:23 says all people have sinned.

Week 6: God Is Love and God Is Just

How can God be both perfectly loving and perfectly just at the same time?

Ella had been wrestling with a question for weeks before she finally put it into words.

'How can God be loving and also punish people? Or send anyone to hell? Those two things do not feel like they fit together.'

Her dad did not answer right away. He thought about it.

'Do you think a judge who lets every guilty person go free is a good person?' he finally asked.

'No,' Ella said. 'That would be terrible. Especially for the victims.'

'Right. So justice is not the opposite of goodness. It is part of it. A good person takes wrong things seriously. They do not look the other way.'

'So God is like that?' Ella said.

'God is perfectly like that. He loves completely. And He is perfectly just. Both of those things are fully true at the same time. And the cross is where you can see them both working together. Jesus took the punishment that justice required. Love provided the rescue that we needed. Both happened at once.'

Ella sat with that for a moment. It did not make the question disappear entirely. But it made more sense than it had before.

God Is Love

First John 4:8 says God is love. This is not simply a description of something He does sometimes. It is a statement about His nature. Love is not a mood God gets into. It is who He is.

John 3:16 shows this love in action. God gave His one and only Son so that whoever believes in Him will not perish but have eternal life.

God's love is not something we earn by being good enough. Romans 5:8 says He demonstrated His love for us in this: while we were still sinners, Christ died for us. He loved us at our worst.

God Is Just

Justice means God always does what is right. He does not ignore wrongdoing. He does not play favorites. He does not let evil slide because it is inconvenient to address.

Deuteronomy 32:4 says all His ways are just. He is a God of faithfulness and without iniquity, just and upright.

For people who have experienced real injustice, this is deeply comforting. Nothing goes unseen. Nothing goes unaddressed forever.

Love and Justice Together

These two attributes are not in tension with each other in God. They work together.

At the cross, justice demanded that sin be paid for. Love stepped in and made the payment. Jesus absorbed the penalty that justice required. That freed God to offer forgiveness to everyone who comes to Him.

Justice was fully satisfied. Love was fully expressed. At the same moment. On the same cross.

Key Verses

"Whoever does not love does not know God, because God is love." (1 John 4:8)

"He is the Rock, his works are perfect, and all his ways are just." (Deuteronomy 32:4)

This Week's Verse to Memorize

1 John 4:8

"Whoever does not love does not know God, because God is love."

God does not just show love. He is love. Write this verse and then write one sentence about what it means that love is not just something God does but who He is.

Activities

Activity 1: Love in Action

Read Romans 5:6-8. Write down what Paul says God did for us and when He did it. Then write one sentence about what this tells you about the nature of God's love.

Activity 2: Justice Matters

Think of a real injustice you have seen or heard about. Write one paragraph about why it matters that God is just. How does knowing God will make all wrongs right affect how you feel about that situation?

Quiz Time

Answer these questions in your journal or workbook:

1. According to 1 John 4:8, what is God?

2. What does Romans 5:8 say about when God showed His love for us?

3. What does it mean that God is just?

4. According to Deuteronomy 32:4, what are all of God's ways?

5. How does the cross show both God's love and God's justice at the same time?

This Week's Challenge

This week, thank God for one specific way He has shown love to you personally. And thank Him for one situation where His justice matters to you. Both prayers, on the same day, will help you hold both truths at once.

New Words to Know

Love: Not primarily a feeling, but a commitment to act for the good of another. God's love is defined by action, most clearly the cross.

Justice: Always doing what is right, including holding wrongdoing accountable. God's justice means no evil goes unaddressed.

Atonement: The satisfaction of God's justice through Jesus's death. It means the debt has been paid.

Wrath: God's settled opposition to everything that is wrong. It is not temper. It is the response of a perfectly just God to evil.

Week 7: Chapter One Review: Putting It All Together

What have you learned about God so far, and how does it all connect?

The final class of the unit was a review day.

Their teacher walked in without any notes. She went to the whiteboard, picked up a marker, and turned to face the class.

'No lecture today,' she said. 'Just tell me what you remember. Anything from the past six weeks.'

The room was quiet for a moment. Then one student raised her hand.

'God does not change.'

The teacher wrote it down.

'Theology means studying God.'

She wrote that too.

'He is holy, holy, holy.'

'He is omniscient, omnipresent, omnipotent.'

'Creation shows us God is real.'

'His love and His justice both show up at the cross.'

By the time the class ran out of things to say, the board was nearly full.

Their teacher stepped back and looked at it. 'Do you know what all of these have in common?' she asked.

Nobody answered.

'They are not just facts,' she said. 'They are descriptions of a person. And a person worth knowing.'

What We Covered in Chapter 1

Six weeks. Six big ideas about who God is. Here is a summary.

Week 1: Theology means the study of God. Asking questions is not a weakness. It is how we grow closer to someone worth knowing.

Week 2: We have good reasons to believe God is real. Creation points to a Creator. Design points to a Designer. And Jesus makes God personally known.

Week 3: God does not change. His character, His Word, His promises, and His love remain completely constant. That makes Him completely trustworthy.

Week 4: God is omniscient, omnipresent, and omnipotent. He knows everything, is everywhere, and can do anything consistent with His character.

Week 5: God is perfectly holy. That holiness is why sin is a real problem and why the gospel is genuinely good news.

Week 6: God is fully loving and fully just. The cross is where both of those truths meet and are satisfied at the same time.

The Foundation Underneath Everything

All six of these truths point in the same direction. God is the kind of being who is actually worth trusting.

He is not unpredictable. He is not distant. He is not weak. He is not cruel. He is not unfair. He is steady, present, powerful, holy, and completely good.

Jeremiah 9:24 says the one thing worth boasting about is knowing and understanding God. Not achievements or possessions. Knowing Him. That is what this whole workbook is about. And you have just laid the foundation.

Key Verses

"Let the one who boasts boast about this: that they have the understanding to know me, that I am the Lord, who exercises kindness, justice, and righteousness on earth." (Jeremiah 9:24)

"The Lord is good, and his love endures forever; his faithfulness continues through all generations." (Psalm 100:5)

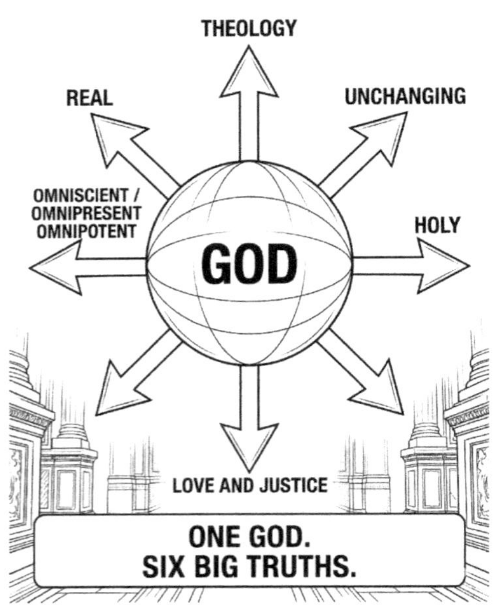

This Week's Verse to Memorize

Jeremiah 9:24

"Let the one who boasts boast about this: that they have the understanding to know me, that I am the Lord."

Knowing God is the thing worth most. Write this verse and then write one sentence about what it means to you personally to know God, not just know about Him.

Activities

Activity 1: Six-Truth Summary

Without looking at your notes, write one sentence for each of the six weeks of this unit describing the main idea. Then write one sentence about which truth has meant the most to you so far and why.

Activity 2: My Questions Revisited

Go back to the list of God questions you wrote in Week 1. Have any of them been answered? Write a short update next to each one. Keep the unanswered ones. You have eleven more units ahead.

Quiz Time

Answer these questions in your journal or workbook:

1. What does theology mean?

2. Name two reasons to believe God is real.

3. What attribute describes God never changing?

4. What are the three omni attributes of God?

5. How do God's love and justice fit together at the cross?

This Week's Challenge

This week, choose the one attribute of God from Unit 1 that you most want to trust more deeply. Write it down and pray about it every day. At the end of the week, write about what changed.

New Words to Know

Review: Looking back at what you have learned to make sure it has settled in.

Foundation: Something you build everything else on. Unit 1 is the theological foundation for the rest of the workbook.

Trustworthy: Reliable and worthy of confidence. All six attributes studied this unit point to God being trustworthy.

Character: The sum of someone's qualities and values. God's character is the reason we can trust all of His promises.

Two

The Trinity

Weeks 8 through 11

Father, Son, and Holy Spirit: One God in three persons. In this unit you will learn who each person is and what they do.

Weeks in this unit:

- Week 8: One God, Three Persons: What Is the Trinity?
- Week 9: God the Father: Creator and Our Perfect Dad
- Week 10: God the Son: Who Is Jesus?
- Week 11: God the Holy Spirit: Helper, Guide, and Power

Week 8: One God, Three Persons: What Is the Trinity?

How can God be three persons and still be one God?

Jordan came home from church with a headache.

Not the kind from a fever. The kind from thinking too hard.

'Dad,' he said, 'my teacher said God is one God. But then the pastor talked about the Father, and Jesus, and the Holy Spirit. That's three. How can three be one?'

His dad put down his book. 'That is one of the best questions anyone can ask about God.'

'But it doesn't make sense,' Jordan said.

'It is hard to fully understand,' his dad said. 'But it is true. And there are some things that help it make more sense. Come sit down, and I will show you.'

What Is the Trinity?

The word Trinity is not found in the Bible. But the idea is on almost every page.

The Trinity means this: there is one God, and He exists as three distinct persons. The Father is God. The Son (Jesus) is God. The Holy Spirit is God. They are not three gods. They are one God in three persons.

All three persons are equal. None is greater or lesser than the others. All three have always existed. And all three are fully God.

Where Do We See the Trinity in the Bible?

One of the clearest places is Jesus's baptism. When Jesus came up out of the water, the Spirit of God came down like a dove. And the Father's voice spoke from heaven, saying, 'This is my Son, whom I love.'

All three persons were there at the same moment. The Son was in the water. The Spirit was descending. The Father was speaking. That is the Trinity in action.

Jesus also told His followers to baptize people 'in the name of the Father and of the Son and of the Holy Spirit' (Matthew 28:19). One name. Three persons.

Wrong Ideas About the Trinity

Over the years, people have come up with ideas that sound helpful but are actually wrong.

Some people say God is like water. Water can be a liquid, ice, or steam. But this idea fails because water is only one thing at a time. God is all three persons at the same time.

Some people say the Father, Son, and Spirit are just different names for the same person. But the Bible shows them talking to each other and acting separately.

The truth is that the Trinity is a mystery. We can learn what the Bible says about it. But we cannot fully wrap our brains around it. That is okay. God is bigger than any idea we could come up with.

Why the Trinity Matters

The Trinity tells us something beautiful about God. God has always been in relationship within Himself. The Father loves the Son. The Son loves the Father. The Spirit is part of that love.

This means God did not create people because He needed someone to love. He was already full of love. He made us to share that love with us.

Knowing God is three in one helps us understand why He is so perfectly complete.

Key Verses

"As soon as Jesus was baptized, he went up out of the water. At that moment, heaven was opened, and he saw the Spirit of God descending like a dove and alighting on him. And a voice from heaven said, This is my Son, whom I love." (Matthew 3:16-17)

"Go and make disciples of all nations, baptizing them in the name of the Father and of the Son and of the Holy Spirit." (Matthew 28:19)

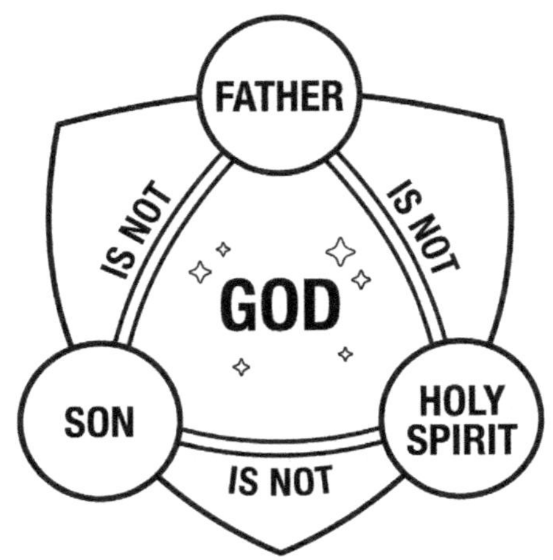

This Week's Verse to Memorize

Matthew 28:19

"Go and make disciples of all nations, baptizing them in the name of the Father and of the Son and of the Holy Spirit."

Notice it says 'in the name,' which is one name, not three names. Write this verse out and circle the word 'name.' What does that tell you?

Activities

Activity 1: Trinity Detectives

Open your Bible to Matthew 3:13-17. Read the story of Jesus's baptism. Find the moment where all three persons of the Trinity appear. Write down who each person is and what they are doing at that moment. You are looking for the Father, the Son, and the Holy Spirit.

Activity 2: Wrong vs. Right

Draw two columns. Label one Wrong Ideas and one What the Bible Says. In the Wrong Ideas column, write the two wrong comparisons from this week's lesson. In the What the Bible Says column, write the correct teaching about the Trinity.

Quiz Time

Answer these questions in your journal or workbook:

1. What does the word Trinity mean?

2. Name all three persons of the Trinity.

3. At Jesus's baptism, which person was in the water, which came down like a dove, and which spoke from heaven?

4. True or False: The Trinity means there are three gods.

5. Why is it okay if we do not fully understand the Trinity?

This Week's Challenge

Try praying a Trinity prayer this week. Start by thanking God the Father for making you. Then thank Jesus for saving you. Then ask the Holy Spirit to help you today. All three persons, one prayer. Write down how it felt to talk to all three.

New Words to Know

Trinity: One God who exists as three distinct persons: Father, Son, and Holy Spirit.

Person (in theology): A distinct individual within the Trinity. Each person is fully God and has His own role.

Modalism: A wrong idea that says Father, Son, and Spirit are just three different names for one person. The Bible shows they are truly distinct.

Week 9: God the Father: Creator and Our Perfect Dad

What does it mean to call God 'Father,' and what does He do?

Ava had heard the words 'Our Father in heaven' her whole life.

She said them every week at church. But one night, she stopped in the middle of the prayer.

'What kind of father is God?' she thought. 'Is he like my dad? Better? Different?'

Her own dad was pretty great. He came to her soccer games. He helped with homework. He told her he loved her.

But she knew some of her friends had dads who were not around. Or who were mean. Or who made promises and forgot them.

She wondered: if your earthly dad is not so great, does that change who God the Father is?

The answer is no. God the Father is not like any earthly dad. He is better. He is perfect. And He never lets you down.

God the Father Created Everything

The first thing the Bible tells us about God is that He is the Creator. Genesis 1:1 says, 'In the beginning, God created the heavens and the earth.'

God the Father made everything that exists. Stars, oceans, mountains, animals, and people. He made it all on purpose. He made it all with care. And He said it was good.

But God the Father did not just make the world and walk away. He keeps it going. He holds it all together. This is called providence. God the Father is always at work in what He made.

God the Father Is Our Perfect Parent

Jesus taught His followers to call God 'Father.' That was actually a big deal. In those days, most people thought of God as distant and powerful. Jesus said you could talk to Him like a dad.

In Romans 8:15, Paul writes that God's Spirit causes us to cry out 'Abba, Father.' Abba is an Aramaic word. It is close to what a small child calls their dad. Daddy. Papa. It is a word of closeness and trust.

God the Father is the perfect parent. He is never too tired to listen. He never forgets you. He never makes promises He does not keep. He disciplines us when we need it, but always with love.

God the Father Is in Control

Sometimes life feels out of control. But God the Father is always in charge.

This does not mean bad things never happen. It means that God sees all of it. He is working even in the hard parts.

Romans 8:28 tells us He causes all things to work together for good for those who love Him.

Trusting God the Father means believing He knows what He is doing, even when we cannot see it.

What If My Earthly Dad Is Not Around?

Some kids grow up without a dad. Some have dads who are not kind or not present. This can make it hard to picture what a good father looks like.

Here is the good news. God the Father is not a reflection of your earthly dad. He is what a perfect father would be. He is everything an earthly dad should be and more.

Psalm 68:5 calls God 'a father to the fatherless.' No matter what your family looks like, God the Father sees you. He knows you. And He wants you.

ABBA, FATHER.

Key Verses

"In the beginning, God created the heavens and the earth." (Genesis 1:1)

"The Spirit you received brought about your adoption to sonship. And by him we cry, Abba, Father." (Romans 8:15)

"A father to the fatherless, a defender of widows, is God in his holy dwelling." (Psalm 68:5)

This Week's Verse to Memorize

Romans 8:15

"The Spirit you received brought about your adoption to sonship. And by him we cry, Abba, Father."

Practice saying Abba, Father slowly three times. This is how close God the Father wants to be with you.

Activities

Activity 1: Compare and Contrast

In your journal, draw two columns. Label one A Perfect Father and one An Earthly Father. Write what makes God the Father perfect in the first column. In the second column, write ways earthly fathers sometimes fall short. At the bottom, write: God the Father is always everything a perfect father would be.

Activity 2: Talk to Your Father

Write a short prayer to God as your Father. Use the word Abba if it feels right. Tell Him one thing you are worried about and one thing you are thankful for. Read it out loud when you are done.

Quiz Time

Answer these questions in your journal or workbook:

1. What does Genesis 1:1 tell us God the Father did?

2. What does the word Abba mean, and why is it important?

3. What is providence?

4. What does Psalm 68:5 call God?

5. True or False: If your earthly dad is not kind, that means God the Father is like that too.

This Week's Challenge

Every morning this week, start the day by saying out loud: 'God is my perfect Father. He sees me. He loves me. He is in control.' Then pause and notice how that changes how you feel before the day begins.

New Words to Know

Providence: God's ongoing care and control over everything He made. He does not just start things and walk away. He stays involved.

Abba: An Aramaic word that means father or daddy. It shows closeness and trust. It is how Jesus described our relationship with God.

Creator: God as the one who made everything out of nothing by His own power and will.

Week 10: God the Son: Who Is Jesus?

Is Jesus just a good teacher, or is He something much more?

A kid at school told Marcus that Jesus was just a great teacher.

'Like Gandhi,' the kid said. 'Or Martin Luther King. A really good person who said wise things.'

Marcus was not sure what to say. Jesus did say wise things. He was good. But was He just a good teacher?

That night, Marcus looked up some of the things Jesus actually said about Himself.

'I am the way and the truth and the life.' (John 14:6)

'Before Abraham was born, I am!' (John 8:58)

'I and the Father are one.' (John 10:30)

Marcus stared at those verses. A good teacher just teaches. He does not claim to be God or say he existed before Abraham. If Jesus said those things and they were not true, He was either lying or out of His mind. But if they were true, He is exactly who He said He was.

Jesus was not just a good teacher. He was making the biggest claim anyone has ever made.

Jesus Is Fully God

The Bible is clear that Jesus is God. John 1:1 says, 'In the beginning was the Word, and the Word was with God, and the Word was God.' Then in verse 14, it says the Word became flesh and made His home among us.

Jesus is not a lesser version of God. He is not a created being. He is the eternal Son of God. Colossians 1:16 says everything was created by Him and for Him.

Jesus also did things only God can do. He forgave sins. He calmed storms. He raised the dead. He rose from the dead Himself. These are not things a regular person does.

Jesus Is Fully Human

Here is the amazing part. Jesus is also fully human.

He was born as a baby. He grew up. He got tired and hungry. He felt emotions. He cried when His friend Lazarus died (John 11:35). He knows what it feels like to be a person.

Hebrews 4:15 says Jesus was tempted in every way just like we are. But He never sinned. Not once.

Jesus being fully human matters a lot. It means He understands our struggles. He is not distant. He has lived this life.

Both at the Same Time

Jesus is not half God and half human. He is 100 percent God and 100 percent human at the same time.

This idea has a big name: the hypostatic union. You do not need to memorize that word. But you do need to understand what it means.

Jesus had two complete natures in one person. His human nature meant He could live the perfect life we could not. His divine nature meant His death could actually pay for our sins.

Both natures were needed. Without His humanity, He could not stand in our place. Without His divinity, His sacrifice would not have been enough.

Why This Changes Everything

When Jesus says He understands you, He really does. He was a kid once. He had hard days. He had people who misunderstood Him.

And when Jesus says He can save you, He really can. He is God. His power has no limit.

Jesus is the only person in history who is both fully human and fully God. That is exactly what we needed.

Key Verses

"In the beginning was the Word, and the Word was with God, and the Word was God... The Word became flesh and made his dwelling among us." (John 1:1, 14)

"For we do not have a high priest who is unable to empathize with our weaknesses, but we have one who has been tempted in every way, just as we are, yet he did not sin." (Hebrews 4:15)

This Week's Verse to Memorize

John 1:14

"The Word became flesh and made his dwelling among us."

This is one of the most important sentences in the Bible. The Word is Jesus. Flesh means He became human. Write it out and put it somewhere you will see it today.

Activities

Activity 1: Gospel Scavenger Hunt

Open the book of Mark, which is the shortest Gospel. Find one story where Jesus does something that shows He is human, like feeling tired or hungry. Then find one story where He does something only God could do. Write down both stories and what they show about Jesus.

Activity 2: What Did Jesus Say About Himself?

Look up these three verses and write them out: John 14:6, John 10:30, and John 8:58. After each verse, write one sentence about what Jesus is claiming. Would a 'just a good teacher' say these things?

Quiz Time

Answer these questions in your journal or workbook:

1. According to John 1:1, who is the Word?

2. Name two things Jesus did that show He is God.

3. Name two things in the Gospels that show Jesus is human.

4. What does it mean that Jesus was tempted but never sinned?

5. Why does it matter that Jesus is both fully God and fully human?

This Week's Challenge

Because Jesus is fully human, He knows exactly how you feel today. Pick one hard thing you are dealing with right now. Then write a short prayer telling Jesus about it. Remember: He has felt hard things too. He is not far away. He gets it.

New Words to Know

Incarnation: God becoming human in the person of Jesus. He did not stop being God. He added a human nature.

Hypostatic Union: The theological term for Jesus having two complete natures, fully God and fully human, in one person.

Sinless: Jesus never once disobeyed God, even though He faced real temptation just like we do.

Week 11: God the Holy Spirit: Helper, Guide, and Power

Who is the Holy Spirit, and is He a real person or just a feeling?

Sofia's Sunday school teacher talked about the Holy Spirit every week.

'The Spirit is moving today,' she would say. Or, 'Let the Spirit lead you.'

Sofia always nodded. But she was not sure what that meant.

Was the Holy Spirit like a feeling? Like goosebumps at church? Was he like the wind? Was he even a real person?

One afternoon, she asked her mom.

'The Holy Spirit is not a feeling,' her mom said. 'He is a real person. He is God. He lives inside every believer. And He does a lot more than give you goosebumps.'

Sofia leaned forward. 'Like what?'

Her mom smiled. 'Let's find out.'

The Holy Spirit Is a Person

A lot of people think of the Holy Spirit as a force or a feeling. Like electricity or a warm glow.

But the Bible describes the Holy Spirit as a person. He has a mind. He has feelings. He makes choices.

We know this because the Bible says He can be grieved (Ephesians 4:30). You cannot grieve a force. You can only grieve a person. The Holy Spirit can be hurt by our wrong choices.

He also teaches (John 14:26), intercedes for us (Romans 8:26), and gives gifts to believers (1 Corinthians 12:11). These are things a person does, not a feeling.

The Holy Spirit Is Fully God

The Holy Spirit is the third person of the Trinity. He is not less than the Father or the Son. He is fully God.

At creation, the Spirit of God was hovering over the waters (Genesis 1:2). He was there from the very beginning. He inspired the writers of the Bible (2 Peter 1:21). He brought Jesus back to life from the dead (Romans 8:11).

The Holy Spirit has always been God, equal with the Father and the Son.

What the Holy Spirit Does for Believers

When someone puts their trust in Jesus, the Holy Spirit comes to live inside them. This is called the indwelling of the Spirit.

Here are some of the things He does in a believer's life.

He convicts us when we do wrong and points us back to God.

He guides us when we have decisions to make.

He comforts us when we are sad or scared.

He gives us power to do what is right.

He helps us understand the Bible when we read it.

Jesus called the Holy Spirit the Counselor (John 14:16). That word means someone who comes alongside you to help. He is always with you.

Pentecost: When the Spirit Came

After Jesus went back to heaven, He promised to send the Spirit. That happened on the Day of Pentecost, described in Acts 2.

The Spirit came like a rushing wind. Tongues of fire appeared. The disciples spoke in languages they had never learned. About three thousand people believed in Jesus that very day.

That same Spirit lives in every believer today. The power at Pentecost is the same power that is available to you right now.

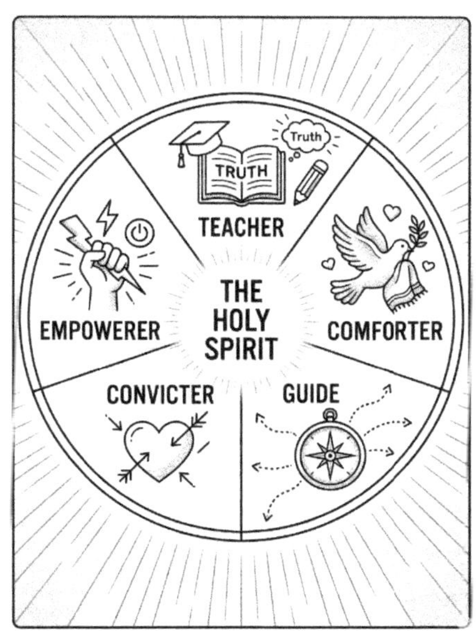

Key Verses

"And I will ask the Father, and he will give you another advocate to help you and be with you forever, the Spirit of truth." (John 14:16-17)

"Do not grieve the Holy Spirit of God, with whom you were sealed for the day of redemption." (Ephesians 4:30)

This Week's Verse to Memorize

John 14:16

"And I will ask the Father, and he will give you another advocate to help you and be with you forever."

The word advocate means helper or one who comes alongside you. Write this verse out. Then underline the word forever. The Spirit never leaves.

Activities

Activity 1: Spirit Roles Card Sort

Write each of the Holy Spirit's five roles on a separate notecard or piece of paper: Teacher, Comforter, Guide, Convicter, Empowerer. Then write one Bible verse next to each role. Use these verses to match them up: John 14:26 (Teacher), John 14:18 (Comforter), Romans 8:14 (Guide), John 16:8 (Convicter), and Acts 1:8 (Empowerer).

Activity 2: Personal Reflection

In your journal, answer this question honestly: Have you ever felt the Holy Spirit doing something in your life? Maybe He helped you choose what was right. Maybe He comforted you when you were sad. Write about what happened.

Quiz Time

Answer these questions in your journal or workbook:

1. True or False: The Holy Spirit is a force or a feeling, not a real person.

2. What does Ephesians 4:30 say we should not do to the Holy Spirit?

3. What does the word indwelling mean?

4. Name three things the Holy Spirit does for believers.

5. What happened on the Day of Pentecost?

This Week's Challenge

Before you make one decision this week, stop and say this prayer: Holy Spirit, I need your help. Please guide me. Then pay attention to what happens. Did you feel nudged toward something? Did a Bible verse come to mind? Did something change? Write about it at the end of the week.

New Words to Know

Indwelling: The Holy Spirit living inside every true believer from the moment they put their trust in Jesus.

Advocate (Paraclete): A Greek word meaning one who comes alongside to help. Jesus used this word to describe the Holy Spirit in John 14.

Pentecost: The day the Holy Spirit was poured out on all believers, as described in Acts 2. This marked the beginning of the church.

Three

The Bible

Weeks 12 through 14

Where did the Bible come from? Can we trust it? And how do we read it well? This unit answers all three questions.

Weeks in this unit:

- Week 12: What Is the Bible and Where Did It Come From?
- Week 13: Can We Trust the Bible?
- Week 14: How to Read and Understand the Bible

Week 12: The Bible

What Is the Bible and Where Did It Come From?

Ella held the Bible in her hands like she was holding something fragile.

It was her great-grandmother's Bible. The cover was worn. The pages were thin. Some of them had handwritten notes in the margins.

'Where did the first Bible come from?' Ella asked her mom. 'Like, who actually wrote it?'

'Lots of people,' her mom said, 'over a long time. But here is what makes it different from any other book. God guided every single word.'

Ella looked down at the old, worn pages. 'So it's really from God?'

'Every bit of it,' her mom said. 'People held the pens. But God gave the message.'

What the Bible Is

The Bible is not just one book. It is a collection of 66 books written by about 40 different authors. Some were kings. Some were fishermen. Some were shepherds. Some were scholars. They lived in different countries and different centuries.

And yet, all 66 books tell one connected story. The story of God and people, from creation all the way to the end of time.

The Bible has two main sections. The Old Testament has 39 books. It covers the story of God's people before Jesus came. The New Testament has 27 books. It covers the life of Jesus and the beginning of the church.

How God Wrote the Bible Through People

The Bible did not fall out of the sky already printed. God worked through real human beings to write it. This process is called inspiration.

Second Timothy 3:16 says, 'All Scripture is God-breathed.' That phrase God-breathed is the key. God breathed His truth into the writers. He used their personalities, their experiences, and their writing styles. But He made sure the message came through without error.

Think of it like this. A musician can play the same song on a piano and a guitar. The instruments are different. The sound is different. But it is still the same song. The Bible's 40 authors are like different instruments. God played the same true song through all of them.

The Bible Took About 1,500 Years to Complete

The first books of the Bible were written around 1400 BC. The last book, Revelation, was written around 95 AD. That means the whole Bible took about 1,500 years to finish.

No group of people sat down and planned it all out. It was written across many generations, many cultures, and many languages. Hebrew, Aramaic, and Greek were the main languages.

And yet the message is consistent from beginning to end. That is one of the strongest signs that one Mind was behind all of it.

The Bible Is Still Being Read Today

The Bible is the most printed book in human history. Some parts of the Bible has been translated into more than 3,500 languages. The full Bible exists in over 700 of them. Billions of people around the world read it every day.

People have tried to destroy it, ban it, and burn it. It has survived all of that. The Bible you hold today is the same message God gave to those first writers thousands of years ago.

Key Verses

"All Scripture is God-breathed and is useful for teaching, rebuking, correcting and training in righteousness." (2 Timothy 3:16)

"For prophecy never had its origin in the human will, but prophets, though human, spoke from God as they were carried along by the Holy Spirit." (2 Peter 1:21)

This Week's Verse to Memorize

2 Timothy 3:16

"All Scripture is God-breathed and is useful for teaching, rebuking, correcting and training in righteousness."

Say this verse slowly. Notice the four things Scripture is useful for: teaching, rebuking, correcting, and training. Which one do you need most right now?

Activities

Activity 1: Bible Map

In your journal, draw a simple timeline. On the left end write 1400 BC. On the right end write 95 AD. Mark where the Old Testament ends and the New Testament begins. Then write the names of three Bible books you know and place them on the timeline based on when you think they were written.

Activity 2: Book Count

Grab your Bible and flip to the table of contents. Count all the books in the Old Testament. Then count all the books in the New Testament. Write the totals in your journal. Then pick one book from each section that you have never read and write down its name as a future reading goal.

Quiz Time

Answer these questions in your journal or workbook:

1. How many books are in the Bible total? How many are in the Old Testament? How many in the New Testament?

2. About how many different authors wrote the Bible?

3. What does the phrase 'God-breathed' mean?

4. What are the three main languages the Bible was originally written in?

5. About how many years did it take to write the whole Bible?

This Week's Challenge

Pick one book of the Bible you have never read before. Start reading it this week, just one or two chapters a day. At the end of the week, write down one thing you learned about God from what you read. The Bible only works if you actually open it.

New Words to Know

Inspiration: The process by which God guided the human authors of the Bible so that what they wrote was exactly what He intended, without error.

Scripture: Another word for the Bible, meaning the holy writings.

Old Testament: The first 39 books of the Bible, written before Jesus was born. They tell the story of God's people and point forward to the coming of Jesus.

New Testament: The last 27 books of the Bible. They record the life of Jesus and the beginning and growth of the Christian church.

Week 13: Can We Trust the Bible?

People say the Bible has been changed over time. How do I know it is still accurate?

Noah's older brother was in high school, and he liked to argue at dinner.

'The Bible has been translated so many times,' his brother said one night. 'It is like a game of telephone. Who knows what the original even said?'

Noah was in fifth grade. He did not know how to argue back. But something about that did not feel right to him.

Later, he asked his dad about it.

'Your brother is thinking of how a normal book gets passed down,' his dad said. 'But the Bible was not passed down casually. It was copied by people who treated it like the most important document in the world. Because they believed it was.'

'So it did not get messed up like a game of telephone?' Noah asked.

'Not at all,' his dad said. 'This is one of the most carefully checked documents in all of history.'

The Telephone Game vs Real Preservation

In the telephone game, one person whispers a message, and it gets passed from person to person. By the end, the message is usually nothing like the original.

Some people think the Bible worked that way. One person wrote it. Then someone copied it. Then someone copied the copy. And so on, for thousands of years.

But that is not how the Bible was preserved. Scholars who study ancient texts have found that Bible copyists worked with extraordinary precision. They counted every word and every letter to make sure nothing was added or left out.

The Dead Sea Scrolls

In 1947, a shepherd boy discovered clay jars in a cave near the Dead Sea. Inside the jars were ancient scrolls, including copies of the Old Testament books that were about 1,000 years older than any copies previously known.

When scholars compared the Dead Sea Scrolls to the copies they already had, the texts were almost identical. A thousand years of copying, and the message had not changed.

The New Testament Is Well Documented

Historians measure ancient documents by how many copies exist and how close in time those copies are to the original.

For most ancient writings, there are only a handful of copies, made hundreds of years after the original. The New

Testament has more than 5,800 ancient Greek manuscripts. The oldest copies were made within decades of the original writings.

Scholars have found small differences between some manuscripts. Most are things like spelling variations. No difference affects any major teaching. Biblical scholars are honest and careful about this work. Their conclusion is that the text we have today is remarkably accurate.

Why the Bible Has Authority

Beyond the historical evidence, Christians believe the Bible is trustworthy because God Himself stands behind it. Jesus quoted the Old Testament as settled truth and said Scripture cannot be broken. (John 10:35.)

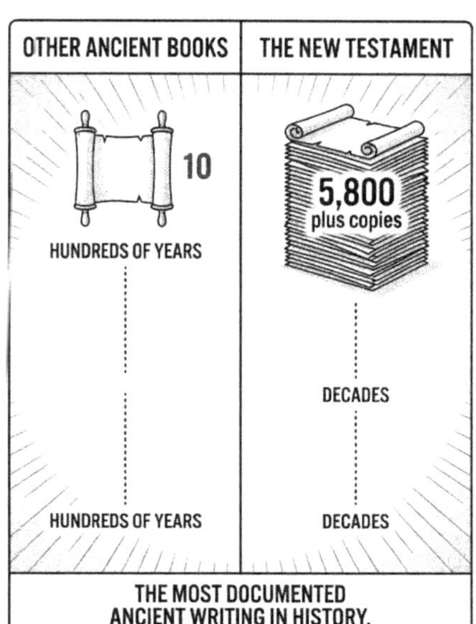

We trust the Bible not just because scholars say it is accurate. We trust it because it is God's Word, and God does not lie. (Titus 1:2.)

Key Verses

"Your word, Lord, is eternal; it stands firm in the heavens." (Psalm 119:89)

"God is not human, that he should lie... Does he speak and then not act? Does he promise and not fulfill?" (Numbers 23:19)

"Scripture cannot be broken." (John 10:35)

This Week's Verse to Memorize

Psalm 119:89

"Your word, Lord, is eternal; it stands firm in the heavens."

Write this verse out and then write one sentence in your own words about what it means. If God's Word stands firm in the heavens, what does that tell you about how dependable it is?

Activities

Activity 1: Be a Text Critic

Play one round of the telephone game with your family. Start with a sentence from the Bible. See how it changes by the end. Then talk about how having thousands of written copies instead of spoken whispers completely changes the reliability of a message.

Activity 2: Look It Up

Search for Dead Sea Scrolls in a children's encyclopedia, a library book, or with a trusted adult online. Write down three facts you did not know before. Share them with your family.

Quiz Time

Answer these questions in your journal or workbook:

1. What is a manuscript?

2. What were the Dead Sea Scrolls, and why were they important?

3. About how many ancient Greek manuscripts of the New Testament exist?

4. True or False: Scholars have found differences between ancient Bible copies that change the main teachings of Christianity.

5. According to John 10:35, what did Jesus say about Scripture?

This Week's Challenge

Find a Bible verse that has meant something to you. Write it on a notecard and keep it somewhere safe. Now think: that same verse was written thousands of years ago, carefully copied by hand by people who wanted to preserve it for future readers. You are holding the end of a very long chain of faithful people. Thank God for it.

New Words to Know

Manuscript: A handwritten copy of a document. Ancient manuscripts of the Bible are stored in museums and libraries around the world.

Textual Criticism: The scholarly work of comparing ancient manuscripts to confirm what the original text said.

Inerrancy: The belief that the Bible, as originally written, is without error in all that it teaches.

Authority: The right to be trusted and obeyed. When we say the Bible has authority, we mean it has the right to tell us what is true and how to live.

Week 14: How to Read and Understand the Bible

The Bible is a big book. How do I actually read it and know what it means?

Grace opened her Bible to a random page and pointed at a verse.

It said: Go, sell everything you have and give to the poor. (Mark 10:21)

She looked at her mom. 'Does that mean I have to give away all my stuff?'

Her mom smiled a little. 'That is a great question. Let me show you something. Who did Jesus say that to?'

Grace read the verses around it. 'A rich young man who asked how to get eternal life.'

'Right,' her mom said. 'Jesus knew that man loved his money more than God. He gave him a specific challenge for a specific situation. Does that mean everyone has to sell everything? Read more of the Bible and see what it says about money and generosity overall.'

'So I have to know who Jesus was talking to before I can know what it means for me?'

'Exactly,' her mom said. 'Context is everything.'

The Bible Is a Library, Not Just a Book

The Bible contains many different kinds of writing. There is history, poetry, letters, prophecy, law, and wisdom literature. Each type works differently and needs to be read differently.

For example, Psalms is a book of poems and songs. Poetry uses pictures and comparisons to express emotion and truth. Reading it like a science textbook will confuse you. Reading it as poetry lets it speak the way it was meant to.

When you read the Bible, it helps to ask: what kind of writing is this? That question guides how you interpret what you are reading.

Context Matters

Context means everything around a verse. Who is speaking? Who are they speaking to? What has happened before this moment in the story?

A verse taken out of context can mean something very different from what the author intended. Reading whole sections, not just individual verses, protects you from misunderstanding.

Here are the main types of writing you will find in the Bible.

History and narrative: Stories of what actually happened, like Genesis, Exodus, and the Gospels.

Law: Rules God gave to His people, like in Leviticus and Deuteronomy.

Poetry and wisdom: Psalms, Proverbs, and Ecclesiastes use poetic language and images.

Prophecy: Messages from God about the future, like Isaiah and Revelation.

Letters: Written to early churches, like Romans, Galatians, and James.

Let Scripture Interpret Scripture

One of the best tools for understanding the Bible is the Bible itself. When a verse is hard to understand, other passages often shed light on it.

Also, read the Bible with the goal of knowing God, not just collecting information. Ask yourself: what does this tell me about who God is? The Holy Spirit, who lives in every believer, helps you understand it.

Key Verses

"Your word is a lamp for my feet, a light on my path." (Psalm 119:105)

"Do your best to present yourself to God as one approved, a worker who does not need to be ashamed and who correctly handles the word of truth." (2 Timothy 2:15)

This Week's Verse to Memorize

Psalm 119:105

"Your word is a lamp for my feet, a light on my path."

Think about walking in complete darkness. A lamp only lights up the next step, not the whole road ahead. How is the Bible like that lamp? Write your answer in your journal.

Activities

Activity 1: What Type Is It?

Look up these five Bible passages. For each one, decide which type of writing it is: History, Law, Poetry, Prophecy, or Letter. Write your answers in your journal.

Genesis 6:9-22

Psalm 23

Leviticus 19:18

Isaiah 9:6

Romans 8:1

Activity 2: Context Detectives

Open to John 11:35, the shortest verse in the English Bible: Jesus wept. Read verses 28 through 44 around it. Answer these questions: Who had died? Why did Jesus weep if He was about to raise Lazarus? What does the context tell you that the two-word verse alone does not?

Quiz Time

Answer these questions in your journal or workbook:

1. Name three types of writing found in the Bible.

2. What does the word context mean?

3. Why is it a problem to read just one verse without reading what is around it?

4. According to Psalm 119:105, what does God's Word do for us?

5. Who helps believers understand the Bible when they read it?

This Week's Challenge

Start a simple reading habit this week. Pick one Gospel: Matthew, Mark, Luke, or John. Read one chapter every day. Before you start each day, say this short prayer: God, please help me understand what you want me to see today. At the end of the week, write down one thing God showed you.

New Words to Know

Context: The verses, chapters, and books surrounding a passage. Understanding context is the key to understanding what a verse actually means.

Genre: The type or category of writing. The Bible contains many genres, including history, poetry, prophecy, law, and letters.

Interpretation: The work of figuring out what a Bible passage means. Good interpretation pays attention to context, genre, and the overall story of the Bible.

Illumination: The Holy Spirit's work of helping believers understand the Bible when they read it.

Make a Difference With Your Review

A Quick Favor Before You Continue

If you have reached this point in the book, you and your child are already doing something important. You are taking time to explore big questions about God, understand Bible truth, and build a strong foundation of faith together.

That matters more than you might realize.

Many parents and teachers search for resources that explain Christian beliefs in a way kids can truly understand. Reviews from families like yours help them discover books that can support their children's faith journey.

Would you be willing to take about 30 seconds to leave a quick review?

You do not need to write a long review. Even a sentence or two helps more families find this book.

You might simply share:

• What your child enjoyed most about the lessons
• How you used the book in your home, classroom, or church
• Something your child learned that surprised you
• Whether the weekly format worked well for your family

Your feedback helps other parents decide if this resource is right for their children.

To leave a review, simply scan the QR code below or visit the link.

https://www.amazon.com/review/create-review/?ie=UTF8&channel=glance-detail&asin=1969357053

Thank you again for investing time in your child's faith and spiritual growth. Your effort to teach them about God, Scripture, and truth will have an impact that lasts far beyond these pages.

With gratitude,

Wonder & Word Press

Helping children understand who God is, what the Bible teaches, and how faith shapes everyday life.

Four

Creation and Humanity

Weeks 15 through 18

Chapter 4 covers four foundational truths about creation and what it means to be human. Each week builds on the one before it.

Weeks in this chapter:

- Week 15: God Made Everything
- Week 16: God Made People Special
- Week 17: Why Are We Here?
- Week 18: Male and Female He Created Them

Week 15: God Made Everything

Did God really make everything, and how did He do it?

Theo loved camping.

One night, far from any city lights, he lay on his back and stared at the sky. He had never seen so many stars.

'How many are there?' he asked his dad.

'Scientists say there are more stars than grains of sand on every beach on Earth,' his dad said.

Theo was quiet for a long time. 'Who made all of them?'

'God did,' his dad said. 'Every single one. And He spoke them into existence. He did not need any materials. He just said the word, and they were there.'

Theo stared up at the vast, dark sky. 'That is the most powerful thing I have ever heard.'

'That is exactly what it is,' his dad said.

God Made Everything Out of Nothing

The very first verse in the Bible says, 'In the beginning, God created the heavens and the earth.' (Genesis 1:1)

Before God created, there was nothing. No matter. No space. No time. Just God.

Theologians have a Latin phrase for this: creation ex nihilo. It means creation out of nothing. God did not use pre-existing materials the way a carpenter uses wood. He spoke, and things came into being that were not there before.

Hebrews 11:3 says, 'The universe was formed at God's command, so that what is seen was not made out of what was visible.' God created the visible world from nothing visible. That is a miracle beyond anything else we know.

The Six Days of Creation

Genesis 1 describes what God made over six days.

Day 1: Light and darkness

Day 2: Sky and water

Day 3: Land, seas, and plants

Day 4: Sun, moon, and stars

Day 5: Fish and birds

Day 6: Land animals and people

After each day, God looked at what He had made and said it was good. After He made people on Day 6, He looked at everything and said it was very good.

God rested on the seventh day. Not because He was tired, but to mark the completion of His work and to set apart a day of rest for His people.

Creation Shows Us What God Is Like

When you look at creation, you see clues about the Creator.

The universe is enormous. That tells us God is incredibly powerful. The world is full of beauty and detail. That tells us God loves beauty and cares about specifics. Living things are complex and precise. That tells us God is wise and orderly.

Psalm 19:1 says, 'The heavens declare the glory of God.' Creation is not just a backdrop. It is a message. Every sunrise, every mountain, every living creature is saying something about the One who made it.

Creation Belongs to God

Because God made everything, everything belongs to Him.

Psalm 24:1 says, 'The earth is the Lord's, and everything in it, the world, and all who live in it.'

This changes how we think about the world. We are not the owners of creation. We are the caretakers. God gave people the job of looking after what He made. That is a big responsibility and a great honor.

Key Verses

"In the beginning, God created the heavens and the earth." (Genesis 1:1)

"The heavens declare the glory of God; the skies proclaim the work of his hands." (Psalm 19:1)

"The earth is the Lord's, and everything in it, the world, and all who live in it." (Psalm 24:1)

This Week's Verse to Memorize

Genesis 1:1

"In the beginning, God created the heavens and the earth."

This is the very first sentence of the Bible. It tells us everything starts with God. Say it out loud five times. Then write it from memory.

Activities

Activity 1: Creation Journal

Go outside for ten minutes. Look carefully at everything around you. Pick five things you see and write them in your journal. Next to each one, write one word that describes what it tells you about God. For example: A flower tells me God loves beauty.

Activity 2: Read Genesis 1

Read all of Genesis 1 in one sitting. As you read, write down every time it says God saw that it was good. How many times does that phrase appear? What does it tell you about how God feels about what He made?

Quiz Time

Answer these questions in your journal or workbook:

1. What does the Latin phrase 'creation ex nihilo' mean?

2. What did God make on Day 3 of creation?

3. What did God say after He made people on Day 6?

4. According to Psalm 19:1, what do the heavens declare?

5. Since God made everything, what does that make us in relation to the world around us?

This Week's Challenge

This week, every time you go outside, take five seconds to look around and say thank you to God for something specific you see. A tree. The sky. Your own hands. By the end of the week, you will have thanked God for dozens of specific things He made. Write down your favorites in your journal.

New Words to Know

Creation ex nihilo: A Latin phrase meaning creation out of nothing. God made the universe without using any pre-existing materials.

Creator: God as the one who made everything that exists, simply by speaking it into being.

Stewardship: The responsibility God gave people to care for the world He made. We are caretakers, not owners, of creation.

Week 16: God Made People Special

What does it mean that God made people in His image?

Jaylen was having a bad day.

A kid at school had told him he was worthless. The word stung more than anything the kid had said before.

That night, Jaylen asked his grandma: 'Am I worth anything?'

His grandma put down her book and looked at him steadily.

'Every human being is made in the image of God,' she said. 'That includes you. That is not a small thing. It is the most important fact about any person you will ever meet.'

Jaylen was quiet.

'What does God say about me?' he asked.

'He says you are very good,' his grandma said. 'He said that the day He made people. And He has not changed His mind.'

Made in the Image of God

Genesis 1:27 says, 'God created mankind in his own image, in the image of God he created them; male and female he created them.'

The Latin phrase for this is imago Dei, which means image of God. Of all the things God made, only people are described this way. Not animals. Not stars. People.

So what does it mean to be made in the image of God? It does not mean we look like God physically. God is spirit. It means something deeper.

What the Image of God Looks Like in Us

Being made in God's image means several things.

We can reason and think. Animals act mostly on instinct. People can reflect, plan, create, and ask questions about meaning.

We can love and form relationships. God is love, and we are made to love others in a way animals simply cannot.

We have a moral sense. We know the difference between right and wrong. That inner sense reflects God's own moral nature.

We are creative. People make art, music, stories, and inventions. This reflects God, who is the original Creator.

We have a spirit that longs for meaning, purpose, and connection with God.

None of these qualities earns us our dignity. We have dignity simply because God made us this way.

What This Means for How We Treat Others

If every person is made in God's image, then every person deserves respect.

This applies to every human being, regardless of age, ability, race, or background. The imago Dei does not belong only to certain people.

When sin entered the world, the image of God was damaged but not destroyed. Every person still carries it. God's plan through Jesus is to restore it fully. Second Corinthians 3:18 says we are being transformed into His image from glory to glory.

Key Verses

"So God created mankind in his own image, in the image of God he created them; male and female he created them." (Genesis 1:27)

"And we all...are being transformed into his image with ever-increasing glory, which comes from the Lord." (2 Corinthians 3:18)

This Week's Verse to Memorize

Genesis 1:27

"So God created mankind in his own image, in the image of God he created them; male and female he created them."

Write this verse and circle the phrase in his own image. Then write one sentence about what it means that God made you to reflect who He is.

Activities

Activity 1: Image of God Inventory

Write down five ways you reflect the image of God. These could be abilities, qualities, or ways you relate to others. For each one, write one sentence about how that quality reflects something true about God.

Activity 2: Who Is Your Neighbor?

Think of three people you know who are very different from you. For each one, write one sentence about how the imago Dei applies to them. How should knowing they are made in God's image change the way you treat them?

Quiz Time

Answer these questions in your journal or workbook:

1. What does the Latin phrase imago Dei mean?

2. According to Genesis 1:27, who was created in God's image?

3. Name three ways humans reflect the image of God.

4. What happened to the image of God in people when sin entered the world?

5. According to 2 Corinthians 3:18, what is happening to believers over time?

This Week's Challenge

This week, every time you are tempted to be unkind to someone, pause and remind yourself: this person is made in the image of God. Write at the end of the week about one moment where that reminder changed how you acted.

New Words to Know

Imago Dei: Latin for image of God. The theological term for the truth that human beings are made to reflect God in a way no other creature is.

Dignity: The inherent worth and value of a person. All human beings have dignity because they are made in the image of God.

Restore: To bring something back to what it was meant to be. God's plan is to restore the image of God in people through Jesus.

Total Depravity: The theological term for how sin affects every part of a person. It does not mean people are as evil as possible, but that sin touches every area of human nature.

Week 17: Why Are We Here? Human Purpose

What is the purpose of human life? Why did God make us?

Nadia stared at a blank piece of paper.

Her teacher had asked the class to answer one question: What is your purpose?

Most of her classmates wrote things like 'to be happy' or 'to be successful.' But none of those felt right to Nadia.

She thought about it all day. At dinner, she asked her parents.

'The Westminster Catechism says it well,' her dad said. 'The purpose of people is to glorify God and enjoy Him forever.'

'What does glorify mean?' Nadia asked.

'It means to show how great God is,' her mom said. 'Everything you do, when you do it well and for the right reasons, can do that.'

Nadia looked at her blank paper. She picked up her pencil and started to write.

Why Are You Here?

Why are you here? This is one of the most important questions a person can ask.

EVERY GIFT POINTS BACK TO THE GIVER.
1 CORINTHIANS 10:31

Lots of people give different answers. Some say the purpose of life is to be happy. Some say it is to be successful. Some say it is to make the world better. These are not wrong exactly. But they are incomplete.

The Bible gives a clear answer. We were created by God, for God, and our purpose is to know Him and live for His glory.

The Westminster Shorter Catechism asks: What is the chief purpose of people? The answer: to glorify God and enjoy Him forever.

What Glorifying God Means

Glorifying God means living in a way that shows how great He is. When you are honest, you reflect His truth. When you are kind, you reflect His love. When you create something beautiful, you reflect His creativity.

Enjoying God means taking delight in who He is. Prayer, worship, and simply being aware of His presence are all ways of enjoying God.

God made people for relationship. He wants to be known by you.

John 17:3 says, 'Now this is eternal life: that they know you, the only true God, and Jesus Christ, whom you have sent.' Knowing God is not just the purpose of eternal life. It begins now.

Your Gifts Are Clues

God gave every person specific abilities and interests. These are clues to how He designed you to reflect His glory.

Are you good at encouraging people? That is a gift for His glory. Are you good at solving problems, making music, or building things? All of it can be done for Him.

Whatever you are good at can be done for God's glory. Your purpose is not one specific career. It is to glorify God in whatever you do.

Key Verses

"Now this is eternal life: that they know you, the only true God, and Jesus Christ, whom you have sent." (John 17:3)

"So whether you eat or drink or whatever you do, do it all for the glory of God." (1 Corinthians 10:31)

This Week's Verse to Memorize

1 Corinthians 10:31

"So whether you eat or drink or whatever you do, do it all for the glory of God."

Even eating and drinking can be done for God's glory. Write this verse and then write one ordinary thing you do every day. How could you do it for God's glory this week?

Activities

Activity 1: What Am I Good At?

Write down five things you are good at or enjoy doing. For each one, write one sentence about how you could use that ability to reflect God's glory. Be specific. Not just 'I could help people' but 'I could use my ability to listen to help a friend who is struggling.'

Activity 2: Purpose Statement

Write a personal purpose statement in two to three sentences. Use what you have learned this week. Start with who made you, include why He made you, and end with what you want to do with that purpose.

Quiz Time

Answer these questions in your journal or workbook:

1. According to the Westminster Shorter Catechism, what is the chief purpose of people?

2. What does it mean to glorify God?

3. What does John 17:3 say eternal life is?

4. How can everyday activities like eating and drinking be done for God's glory?

5. Why are your specific gifts and abilities clues to your purpose?

This Week's Challenge

Choose one thing you do this week, a school assignment, a chore, a sport, or a hobby, and do it intentionally for God's glory. Before you start, say: I am doing this for You. Write at the end of the week about whether it changed how you approached it.

New Words to Know

Glorify: To show how great something or someone is. We glorify God when we live in a way that reflects who He is.

Westminster Catechism: A summary of Christian teaching written in 1647. It begins with the question: What is the chief purpose of people?

Vocation: A calling. The idea that God has given each person specific gifts and a specific place to use them for His glory.

Eternal Life: In the Bible, eternal life is not just life that goes on forever. It is knowing God personally. (John 17:3.)

Week 18: Male and Female He Created Them

Why did God make people as male and female, and what does that mean?

Rosa and her twin brother Carlos had argued about who was better at things their whole lives.

Carlos was faster. Rosa was stronger. Carlos was better at math. Rosa was better at writing. Carlos was funnier. Rosa was a better listener.

One day their mom smiled at both of them. 'You know, God made you different on purpose. Not so one of you could win. So that together, you could do more than either of you could alone.'

Rosa thought about that. She and Carlos were different. But they were equally loved by their parents. Equally important in the family.

'God works that way too,' her mom said. 'He made male and female different. But both equally in His image. Both equally loved. Both equally needed.'

God Made Two Kinds of People

Genesis 1:27 says, 'God created mankind in his own image, in the image of God he created them; male and female he created them.'

Male and female are not accidents. They are not cultural ideas. They are part of God's intentional design from the very beginning.

God looked at everything He had made, including people as male and female, and said it was very good. That means both being male and being female is something God called good.

Equal in Dignity

One of the clearest teachings in the Bible is that men and women are equally made in God's image. Neither is more human than the other. Neither is more valuable than the other.

Galatians 3:28 says, 'There is neither Jew nor Gentile, neither slave nor free, nor is there male and female, for you are all one in Christ Jesus.'

This verse is talking about spiritual equality before God. Every person, regardless of their background or sex, has equal standing before Him. Equal dignity. Equal worth. Equal access to His love and salvation.

Different but Complementary

Equal in dignity does not mean identical. God made men and women to be different in ways that complement each other.

The word complementary means that two different things fit together and bring out the best in each other. A lock and a key are different. But they work together perfectly.

From the very beginning, God said it was not good for the man to be alone (Genesis 2:18). He made woman as a helper and partner. The word helper here does not mean lesser. In the Bible, God Himself is often called a helper. It means one who comes alongside to complete what is lacking.

Why This Matters for How We Live

Understanding that God made male and female with purpose helps us in a few important ways.

First, it tells us that your sex is not a mistake. Being a boy or a girl is part of how God designed you. It is good.

Second, it tells us to treat everyone with equal respect. Boys and girls are different, but they are equally valuable. Neither gets to look down on the other.

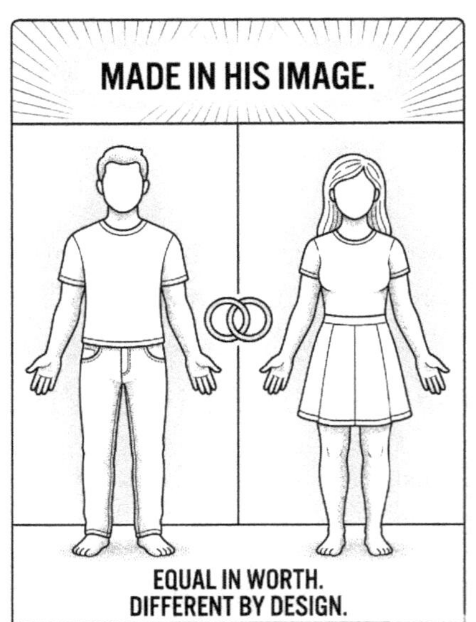

Third, it tells us that men and women need each other. Our differences are gifts, not problems. When we respect those differences, families, friendships, and communities are stronger.

God saw everything He had made, including this design, and called it very good.

Key Verses

"So God created mankind in his own image, in the image of God he created them; male and female he created them." (Genesis 1:27)

"There is neither Jew nor Gentile, neither slave nor free, nor is there male and female, for you are all one in Christ Jesus." (Galatians 3:28)

This Week's Verse to Memorize

Galatians 3:28

"There is neither Jew nor Gentile, neither slave nor free, nor is there male and female, for you are all one in Christ Jesus."

This verse lists three kinds of differences and says none of them change our standing before God. Write it out and underline the phrase 'all one in Christ Jesus.' What does that phrase mean to you?

Activities

Activity 1: Complementary Pairs

In your journal, list five pairs of things that are different but work together well. For example: a left hand and a right hand. A question and an answer. Rain and sunshine. Write down what each pair accomplishes together that neither could do alone. Then think about how this picture applies to men and women.

Activity 2: Equal Worth

Look up Galatians 3:28 in your Bible and read the verses around it. Write down in your own words what Paul is trying to say. Then answer this question: if all people have equal worth before God, how should that change the way we treat people who are different from us?

Quiz Time

Answer these questions in your journal or workbook:

1. According to Genesis 1:27, who did God create as male and female?

2. What does the word 'complementary' mean?

3. According to Galatians 3:28, are men and women equal before God?

4. What does it mean that being a boy or girl is part of God's design?

5. True or False: Equal in dignity means that men and women are identical in every way.

This Week's Challenge

Think of one person in your life who is different from you, whether that is a different age, background, or personality. This week, do one specific thing to show that you value them. Write a note, do something kind, or simply take time to listen to them. Every person is made in God's image and deserves to be treated that way.

New Words to Know

Complementary: Two things that are different in ways that fit together well and bring out the best in each other. Men and women were designed to complement each other.

Equality: Having the same worth and dignity. Men and women have equal dignity before God even though they are different.

Helper: In Genesis 2, the role God gave the woman in relation to the man. In the Bible, being a helper is a position of strength and importance. God Himself is called a helper in Psalm 121:2.

Five

Sin and the Fall

Weeks 19 through 21

What is sin? How did it enter the world? And why does it still affect everything? This unit answers all three questions and ends pointing to hope.

Weeks in this unit:

- Week 19: What Is Sin?
- Week 20: The Fall
- Week 21: How Sin Affects Everything

Week 19: What Is Sin?

Everyone talks about sin. But what exactly is it?

Marcus knew he had done something wrong the moment he said it.

He had made fun of a kid in his class in front of everyone. The kid's face went red. He looked down at his shoes. Marcus felt a twist in his stomach.

He told himself it was not a big deal. Just a joke. But it kept bothering him all afternoon.

That night, he told his dad what happened.

'Why do you think it bothered you so much?' his dad asked.

Marcus thought about it. 'Because I knew it was wrong. Even while I was doing it.'

His dad nodded. 'That feeling is important. It is your conscience telling you that you missed the mark. That is actually one of the ways the Bible describes sin. Missing the mark. Falling short of what we were made to be.'

What the Word Sin Actually Means

The most common word for sin in the New Testament is a Greek word, hamartia. It means to miss the mark. Like an archer who aims at a target but shoots wide. The arrow goes somewhere, but not where it was supposed to go.

Sin is not just doing something obviously terrible. Sin is any thought, word, or action that falls short of what God made us to be and do.

The Bible uses several different words to describe sin. Each one captures a different angle of the same problem.

Missing the mark: Falling short of God's standard. (Romans 3:23 says all have sinned and fall short of the glory of God.)

Transgression: Crossing a line. Stepping over a boundary God has set.

Iniquity: Twisted or crooked behavior. Acting in ways that are bent away from what is right.

Rebellion: Deliberately choosing to go our own way instead of God's way.

Sin Is About Relationship, Not Just Rules

It is easy to think of sin as breaking a list of rules. But that misses the heart of it.

Sin is first and foremost a problem in our relationship with God. When we sin, we are not just breaking a rule. We are turning away from a Person who loves us and knows what is best for us.

Think of it this way. If you lie to a stranger, it is wrong. But if you lie to your best friend, it hurts the relationship in a deeper way. Sin works like that with God. It is not just a rule violation. It damages something precious.

Sin Starts in the Heart

Jesus said in Matthew 15:19 that evil thoughts, murder, adultery, theft, false witness, and slander all come from the heart. Sin does not start with what we do. It starts with what we want and what we think.

This is why simply trying harder to behave does not fix the sin problem. The problem goes deeper than behavior. It starts inside.

The good news is that God knows this. And His solution goes just as deep. He does not just ask us to change our behavior. He offers to change our hearts. That is what the rest of this workbook is building toward.

Key Verses

"For all have sinned and fall short of the glory of God." (Romans 3:23)

"If we claim to be without sin, we deceive ourselves and the truth is not in us." (1 John 1:8)

This Week's Verse to Memorize

Romans 3:23

"For all have sinned and fall short of the glory of God."

The word 'all' in this verse includes you, your parents, your pastor, and every person who has ever lived except Jesus. Write this verse out and then write one sentence about what it means that no one is left out.

Activities

Activity 1: Four Words for Sin

In your journal, draw four boxes. Label them: Missing the Mark, Transgression, Iniquity, Rebellion. In each box, write a simple example of what that kind of sin might look like in everyday life. Use situations from your own experience, like school, sports, or friendships.

Activity 2: Where Does It Start?

Read Matthew 15:17-20. In your journal, make two columns. Label the first column Outside and the second column Inside. Write down two things people often think make someone sinful and put them in the Outside column. Then write down what Jesus says actually causes sinful behavior and put those in the Inside column. What does this tell you about where change needs to start?

Quiz Time

Answer these questions in your journal or workbook:

1. What does the Greek word 'hamartia' mean?

2. Name three different words the Bible uses to describe sin.

3. Is sin only about breaking rules? What else is it about?

4. According to Jesus in Matthew 15:19, where does sin come from?

5. According to Romans 3:23, who has sinned?

This Week's Challenge

This week, when you do something you know is wrong, stop and name it honestly. Do not make excuses or blame someone else. Just say: that was a sin, and it matters. Then ask God to forgive you and help you do better. Honest confession is the first step toward change.

New Words to Know

Sin: Any thought, word, or action that falls short of God's standard and damages our relationship with Him.

Hamartia: The Greek word most often translated sin in the New Testament. It means to miss the mark.

Conscience: The inner sense that tells us when we have done something wrong. God built it into us as part of bearing His image.

Transgression: One of the Bible's words for sin, meaning to cross a boundary or step over a line God has set.

Week 20: The Fall

How did sin get into the world in the first place?

Lily could not stop thinking about the cookies.

Her mom had said clearly: do not eat the cookies on the counter. They were for the school bake sale tomorrow.

But the more Lily told herself no, the more she wanted one.

She thought, just one will not hurt. Mom probably will not notice. I deserve a treat.

She ate one. Then another.

When her mom came home and saw the half-empty plate, Lily felt sick. Not from the cookies. From what she had done.

'Why?' her mom asked quietly.

Lily could not really explain it. She had known it was wrong. She had done it anyway. And now something had changed between her and her mom. It was small, but it was there.

That small moment is a picture of something much bigger that happened at the very beginning of human history.

The Garden and the Choice

Genesis 2 and 3 tell the story of the first people, Adam and Eve, in the Garden of Eden. God placed them in a perfect place. They had everything they needed. Their relationship with God was open and unbroken.

God gave them one command. They could eat from any tree in the garden except one: the tree of the knowledge of good and evil. God told them clearly that eating from it would bring death.

Then a serpent came and questioned God's word. He told Eve that God was holding something back from her. That eating the fruit would not bring death but would make her wise like God.

Eve listened. She ate. She gave some to Adam. He ate too.

What Changed Immediately

The moment they ate, everything changed.

Genesis 3:7 says their eyes were opened and they felt shame for the first time. They hid from each other. Then they hid from God.

When God came to walk with them in the garden as He had done before, they were nowhere to be found. For the first time in human history, people were hiding from the God who loved them.

That hiding, that shame, that broken relationship, is what the Bible calls the Fall. Humanity fell from the good and open relationship with God that we were made for.

The Consequences

God did not ignore what had happened. There were real consequences.

The relationship between people and God was broken. Sin creates separation.

Work and life became harder. The world itself was affected by the Fall.

Physical death entered the world. God had warned them, and He was telling the truth.

Spiritual death also entered. Being spiritually dead means being cut off from the life of God.

Romans 5:12 says, 'Sin entered the world through one man, and death through sin, and in this way death came to all people, because all sinned.'

But God Did Not Walk Away

Here is the most important thing about Genesis 3. Even after the Fall, God came looking for Adam and Eve. He called out, 'Where are you?' (Genesis 3:9)

He was not surprised. He was not defeated. And right there in the middle of the consequences, God made a promise. In Genesis 3:15, He said that one day someone would come who would crush the serpent's head. That is the first hint in the whole Bible of Jesus.

The Fall is a dark chapter. But God was already writing the rescue story before the chapter even ended.

Key Verses

"Therefore, just as sin entered the world through one man, and death through sin, and in this way death came to all people, because all sinned."

(Romans 5:12)

"But God demonstrates his own love for us in this: While we were still sinners, Christ died for us." (Romans 5:8)

This Week's Verse to Memorize

Romans 5:8

"But God demonstrates his own love for us in this: While we were still sinners, Christ died for us."

Notice the word 'while.' God did not wait for us to get better before He sent help. He acted while we were still in the problem. Write this verse out and circle the word 'while.'

COMMUNION IN THE GARDEN

THE FALL - ISOLATION

Activites

Activity 1: Read Genesis 3

Read all of Genesis 3. As you read, write down three things that changed the moment Adam and Eve ate the fruit. Then write down one thing that did NOT change, based on how God responded.

Activity 2: The First Promise

Look up Genesis 3:15. This is sometimes called the Protoevangelium, which means the first gospel. Read it carefully. Who does God say will crush the serpent? Write in your journal why you think this verse is considered the first hint of Jesus in the whole Bible.

Quiz Time

Answer these questions in your journal or workbook:

1. What was the one thing God told Adam and Eve not to do in the garden?

2. What did the serpent tell Eve that was a lie?

3. What did Adam and Eve do immediately after eating the fruit?

4. Name two consequences of the Fall.

5. What promise did God make in Genesis 3:15, and who does it point to?

This Week's Challenge

Think about a time when you hid something wrong you had done. Maybe you hid it from a parent, a friend, or from God. This week, practice the opposite of hiding. If there is something you have been keeping hidden, bring it into the open. Tell God about it in prayer. If it involves another person, consider whether you need to apologize. Hiding keeps us stuck. Honesty starts the healing.

New Words to Know

The Fall: The event in Genesis 3 when Adam and Eve disobeyed God, resulting in sin and death entering the world and humanity's relationship with God being broken.

Spiritual Death: Being cut off from the life of God. Not physical dying, but a state of separation from Him.

Protoevangelium: A Latin word meaning the first gospel. It refers to Genesis 3:15, which is the first hint in the Bible of the coming of Jesus to defeat sin.

Consequence: A result that follows from an action. Sin has real consequences because God is just and truthful.

Week 21: How Sin Affects Everything

If I did not personally sin in the Garden of Eden, why am I affected by it?

Zach's grandpa had a heart condition. It ran in the family.

Zach was only eleven. He had never had any heart problems. But his doctor still wanted him to be tested.

'Why do I have to worry about this now?' Zach asked his mom. 'I feel totally fine.'

'Because the condition is already in your genes,' his mom said. 'You inherited it. You did not choose it. But it is still real, and it is still something we need to pay attention to.'

Zach thought about that. He had not done anything to deserve the condition. It just came with being part of the family.

Sin works a little like that. Not exactly the same. But the idea that something serious can be inherited, something you did not personally choose but still affects you, is one way to begin understanding what the Bible calls original sin.

We Are All Born Into a Broken World

When Adam and Eve sinned, the effects did not stay with just them. The brokenness spread to all of humanity.

Psalm 51:5 says, 'Surely I was sinful at birth, sinful from the time my mother conceived me.' David was not saying he had done terrible things as a newborn. He was saying the tendency toward sin was present from the very beginning of his life.

This tendency is called a sin nature. We do not have to be taught how to be selfish or dishonest. Those tendencies come naturally.

What Total Depravity Means

Theologians use the phrase total depravity to describe how far sin reaches into human nature. It does not mean every person is as evil as possible. It means sin has affected every part of us.

Our minds do not naturally seek God. We tend to think about ourselves first.

Our desires are often aimed at wrong things. We want what we should not want.

Our wills resist God. Doing what is right does not come naturally on our own.

Romans 3:10-11 says, 'There is no one righteous, not even one; there is no one who understands; there is no one who seeks God.'

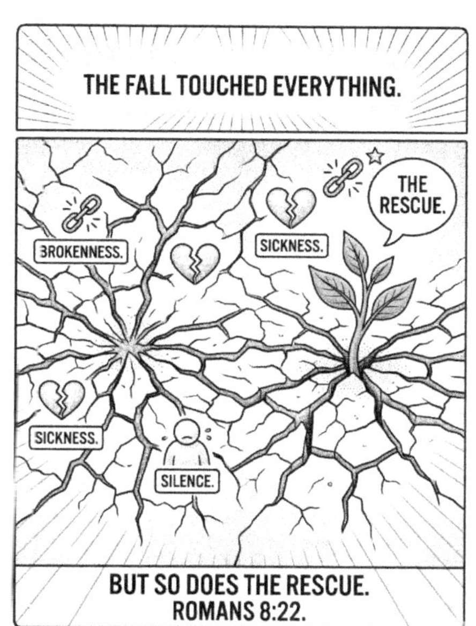

Sin Affected All of Creation

The Fall did not just affect people. It affected creation itself. Romans 8:20-22 says the whole creation was subjected to frustration and has been groaning as if in the pains of childbirth.

This is why the world has suffering, disease, and death. These are not part of God's original design. They are consequences of the Fall.

Understanding the depth of sin is not meant to make you feel hopeless. It is meant to help you understand why the rescue Jesus provides is so significant. Sin is deep. The solution has to be just as deep. And it is.

Key Verses

"Surely I was sinful at birth, sinful from the time my mother conceived me." (Psalm 51:5)

"There is no one righteous, not even one; there is no one who understands; there is no one who seeks God." (Romans 3:10-11)

This Week's Verse to Memorize

Romans 3:23

"For all have sinned and fall short of the glory of God."

The word all leaves no exceptions. Write this verse and then write one sentence about why it matters that everyone is included in this, not just obviously bad people.

Activities

Activity 1: Evidence of the Fall

Look at the news or think about your week. Write down three examples of brokenness in the world: things that are clearly not the way they were meant to be. For each one, write one sentence about how it connects to what you have learned about the Fall.

Activity 2: Deep Problem, Deep Solution

This unit ends with sin. But Unit 6 is all about the rescue. Write a short paragraph predicting: if sin is this deep and this widespread, what kind of solution would be big enough to fix it? Save what you write and compare it to what you learn in Unit 6.

Quiz Time

Answer these questions in your journal or workbook:

1. What is a sin nature?

2. What does total depravity mean? What does it NOT mean?

3. According to Romans 3:10-11, how many people are naturally righteous?

4. How did the Fall affect creation beyond just people?

5. Why is understanding the depth of sin important for understanding the gospel?

This Week's Challenge

This week, notice one moment when your sin nature shows up without you choosing it: an automatic selfish reaction, a quick jealous thought, an impulse to be unkind. Do not beat yourself up about it. Just notice it and bring it to God. Write about what you noticed at the end of the week.

New Words to Know

Original Sin: The theological term for the inherited sinfulness that all people are born with as a result of Adam and Eve's sin.

Sin Nature: The inborn tendency toward sin that every person has. It does not excuse sin but explains why it comes so naturally.

Total Depravity: The teaching that sin affects every part of a person. It does not mean maximum evil but pervasive influence.

Redemption: Being bought back or rescued. Unit 6 covers how God provides this rescue through Jesus.

Six

Salvation and the Gospel

Weeks 22 through 25

What is the gospel? What did Jesus do? How are we saved? And what does salvation give us? The heart of the whole workbook.

Weeks in this chapter:

- Week 22: What Is the Gospel?
- Week 23: Who Is Jesus and What Did He Do?
- Week 24: How Are We Saved?
- Week 25: What Does Salvation Give Us?

Week 22: What Is the Gospel?

Everyone says the gospel is good news. But what exactly is the news?

Mia had heard the word gospel her whole life.

It was in songs, in sermons, on the sign outside her church.

But one day, a friend at school asked her what it meant, and Mia realized she could not explain it.

She knew it was good news. But good news about what?

That night, she asked her dad.

'The gospel is the best news anyone has ever heard,' he said. 'It goes like this. God made us for a relationship with Him. Sin broke that relationship. We could not fix it ourselves. So God sent Jesus to fix it for us. Jesus lived the perfect life we could not live. He died to take the punishment we deserved. Then He rose from the dead to prove that death does not have the final word. And now anyone who trusts in Him is forgiven and brought back to God.'

Mia was quiet for a moment.

'That is the whole thing?' she asked.

'That is the whole thing,' her dad said. 'Four moves. Creation. Fall. Rescue. Restoration.'

Gospel Means Good News

The word gospel comes from an old English word that means good news. In the original Greek of the New Testament, the word is euangelion. It was used in the ancient world when a messenger arrived with news of a great victory.

The Christian gospel is exactly that. It is an announcement. Something has happened. The battle has been won. The rescue has been accomplished.

The Four-Part Story

The gospel makes the most sense when you see it as a four-part story.

- **Creation**: God made everything good. He made people to know Him and enjoy Him.
- **Fall**: People sinned. That sin broke our relationship with God and brought death into the world.
- **Rescue**: God sent Jesus. Jesus lived, died, and rose again to deal with sin and restore what was broken.
- **Restoration**: One day God will make everything new. And right now, anyone who trusts Jesus begins that new life.

Every part of the Bible fits somewhere in this story. Every book, every verse, every promise points to one of these four movements.

The Gospel Is an Announcement, Not a To-Do List

Here is one of the most important things to understand about the gospel. It is not a list of things you need to do. It is news about something that has already been done.

Jesus said from the cross, 'It is finished.' (John 19:30) That means the work of rescue is complete. We do not add to it. We receive it.

First Corinthians 15:3-4 gives the core of the gospel in one sentence: 'Christ died for our sins according to the Scriptures, he was buried, he was raised on the third day according to the Scriptures.'

That is the gospel. Death, burial, resurrection. Sin dealt with. Death defeated.

Key Verses

"For I delivered to you as of first importance what I also received: that Christ died for our sins in accordance with the Scriptures, that he was buried, that he was raised on the third day in accordance with the Scriptures." (1 Corinthians 15:3-4)

"It is finished." (John 19:30)

This Week's Verse to Memorize

1 Corinthians 15:3-4

"Christ died for our sins according to the Scriptures, he was buried, he was raised on the third day according to the Scriptures."

This is the shortest, clearest summary of the gospel in the whole Bible. Three facts: died, buried, raised. Write it out and say it from memory.

Activities

Activity 1: The Four-Part Story

Draw a simple four-panel comic strip in your journal. Label the panels: Creation, Fall, Rescue, Restoration. In each panel, draw a simple image and write one sentence that captures what happened in that part of the story. You now have the entire Bible summarized in four panels.

Activity 2: Gospel in One Sentence

Write the gospel in exactly one sentence using your own words. No more than 25 words. Then share it with someone in your family and see if they have questions. Try to answer them using what you learned this week.

Quiz Time

Answer these questions in your journal or workbook:

1. What does the word 'gospel' mean?

2. What are the four parts of the gospel story?

3. Is the gospel a list of things to do, or news about something already done?

4. What does Jesus mean when He says 'It is finished' in John 19:30?

5. According to 1 Corinthians 15:3-4, what are the three core facts of the gospel?

This Week's Challenge

This week, practice explaining the gospel to someone. Start by writing it out yourself using the four parts. Then try saying it out loud. The goal is to know the gospel well enough to share it naturally.

New Words to Know

Gospel: A Greek word meaning good news. The Christian gospel is the announcement that Jesus died for our sins and rose again.

Euangelion: The original Greek word for gospel. It means a message of great victory or good news.

Atonement: The work Jesus did on the cross to deal with sin and restore the relationship between people and God.

Week 23: Who Is Jesus and What Did He Do?

Why did Jesus have to be the one to save us? Could anyone else have done it?

Daniel had a question that had been bothering him for weeks.

'Why did it have to be Jesus?' he asked his Sunday school teacher. 'Why could God not just forgive everyone without someone dying?'

His teacher thought for a moment.

'Good question,' she said. 'Think about it this way. If someone breaks your window, sorry is not enough. The window still needs to be fixed. Someone has to pay for it.'

'So sin is like a broken window?' Daniel asked.

'Sin is much more serious than that,' she said. 'But the idea is right. Sin has a cost. God is just, which means He does not simply look the other way. The cost had to be paid. And because we could not pay it, Jesus paid it for us.'

'Why Jesus specifically?' Daniel asked.

'Because only someone who was fully human could represent us. And only someone who was fully God could bear the full weight of what sin deserved. Jesus was both. That is why only He could do what needed to be done.'

The Incarnation

The word incarnation means God becoming flesh. John 1:14 says, 'The Word became flesh and made his dwelling among us.'

Jesus did not stop being God when He became human. He was fully God and fully human at the same time. We talked about this in Week 10. It is called the hypostatic union.

Why did it matter? Because the rescue had to come from inside the human family. Jesus became one of us so He could stand in for us.

The Perfect Life

Before Jesus could die for our sins, He had to live a life without any sin of His own.

Hebrews 4:15 says He was tempted in every way we are, yet He never sinned. He did not die for His own sin. He had none. He died for ours.

His perfect life is not just impressive. It is essential to the rescue.

The Cross

On the cross, Jesus took the punishment our sin deserved.

Second Corinthians 5:21 says God made Jesus, who had no sin, to be sinless for us, so that we might become the righteousness of God.

Our sins went to Jesus. His righteousness comes to us. Theologians call this the great exchange.

The Resurrection

Three days after He was buried, Jesus rose from the dead. This is a historical fact that the early church staked everything on.

The resurrection proves Jesus is who He claimed to be. It proves death is not the end. And it guarantees that everyone who trusts in Jesus will also be raised.

First Corinthians 15:17 says, 'If Christ has not been raised, your faith is futile.' The resurrection is not optional. It is the whole point.

Key Verses

"God made him who had no sin to be sin for us, so that in him we might become the righteousness of God." (2 Corinthians 5:21)

"The Word became flesh and made his dwelling among us." (John 1:14)

This Week's Verse to Memorize

2 Corinthians 5:21

"God made him who had no sin to be sin for us, so that in him we might become the righteousness of God."

This verse describes the great exchange. Jesus took our sin. We receive His righteousness. Write it out and circle what Jesus took and what we receive.

Activities

Activity 1: The Great Exchange

Draw a simple diagram in your journal. On the left, write: What we brought to the cross. On the right, write: What we received from the cross. Fill in both sides based on what you learned this week. Then write one sentence explaining why this exchange was only possible because Jesus was both fully God and fully human.

Activity 2: Why the Resurrection Matters

Read 1 Corinthians 15:12-20. Paul lists several things that would be true if Jesus had not risen. Write down three of them. Then write down three things that are true because He did rise.

Quiz Time

Answer these questions in your journal or workbook:

1. What does the word 'incarnation' mean?

2. Why did it matter that Jesus lived a perfect, sinless life?

3. What happened on the cross in terms of the exchange between Jesus and us?

4. What does the resurrection prove?

5. According to 1 Corinthians 15:17, what would be true if Jesus had not risen?

This Week's Challenge

Find one person this week and tell them one fact about what Jesus did. It can be about the incarnation, the cross, or the resurrection. Just one fact, told simply and honestly. See what they say.

New Words to Know

Incarnation: The event of God becoming human in the person of Jesus Christ. From the Latin word for flesh.

Substitution: When someone takes the place of another. Jesus died as our substitute, taking the punishment we deserved.

Resurrection: Jesus rising from the dead three days after His crucifixion. This is the central historical claim of Christianity.

The Great Exchange: The transaction at the cross: our sin was placed on Jesus, and His righteousness is credited to us.

Week 24: How Are We Saved?

What do I actually have to do to be saved?

Sophie had been going to church her whole life. She knew the stories. She knew the songs.

But she was not sure she was actually saved.

'What does it actually take?' she asked her mom one evening.

'Three things work together,' her mom said. 'Hearing the truth about Jesus. Turning from sin. And trusting Jesus personally.'

'Is that all?' Sophie asked. 'I thought I had to be good enough.'

'That is the thing,' her mom said. 'You can never be good enough. None of us can. That is the whole point of grace. Grace means God gives us what we do not deserve and could never earn.'

'So it is not about being good?'

'Being good matters,' her mom said. 'But it is the result of being saved, not the cause of it. You do not get saved by being good. You become good because you are saved.'

Grace: The Starting Point

Ephesians 2:8-9 says, 'For it is by grace you have been saved, through faith, and this is not from yourselves, it is the gift of God, not by works, so that no one can boast.'

Grace means getting what we do not deserve. God offers salvation as a free gift. It cannot be earned by going to church, being kind, or following rules.

This does not make those things unimportant. It means they are responses to salvation, not the cause of it.

Faith: How We Receive It

Faith is how we receive the gift of grace. But faith is not just believing facts. Even demons believe that God exists (James 2:19).

Saving faith has three parts. First, knowing who Jesus is and what He did. Second, agreeing it is true. Third, personally trusting Jesus, not just agreeing with information about Him.

Think of a chair. You can believe a chair will hold you. But faith means actually sitting down in it.

Repentance: Turning Around

Repentance means turning. It is a change of direction.

To repent is to recognize that you have been going your own way, that it leads somewhere bad, and to turn toward God instead.

Repentance is not just feeling sorry. You can feel sorry and keep doing the same thing. Repentance is a genuine change in direction. Acts 3:19 says, 'Repent and turn to God, so that your sins may be wiped out.'

Faith and repentance always go together. You cannot truly trust Jesus without also turning from the sin He died to free you from.

What About Baptism and Church?

Baptism and being part of a church are both important. But they do not save you.

Baptism is a public declaration of what has already happened inside. It is a symbol of dying to sin and rising to new life.

Salvation happens between you and God, by grace through faith, with a heart turned toward Him.

Key Verses

"For it is by grace you have been saved, through faith, and this is not from yourselves, it is the gift of God, not by works, so that no one can boast." (Ephesians 2:8-9)

"Repent and turn to God, so that your sins may be wiped out." (Acts 3:19)

This Week's Verse to Memorize

Ephesians 2:8-9

"For it is by grace you have been saved, through faith, and this is not from yourselves, it is the gift of God, not by works, so that no one can boast."

This verse rules out pride completely. No one can boast about being saved because no one earned it. Write it out and underline the words 'gift of God.'

Activities

Activity 1: Grace, Faith, Repentance

In your journal, draw three columns labeled Grace, Faith, and Repentance. Write a one-sentence definition of each in your own words. Then write one sentence explaining how the three work together when a person is saved.

Activity 2: The Chair Illustration

Write about a time in your own life when you had to move from just believing something to actually trusting it. How is that like having faith in Jesus.

Quiz Time

Answer these questions in your journal or workbook:

1. What does the word 'grace' mean?
2. According to Ephesians 2:8-9, can salvation be earned by good works?
3. What are the three parts of saving faith?
4. What is repentance? How is it different from just feeling sorry?
5. Does baptism save a person? Explain.

This Week's Challenge

Have an honest conversation with God this week. Tell Him what you understand about the gospel. Tell Him where you are with faith and repentance. If you have already trusted Jesus, thank Him for the grace you did not deserve. If you are still working it out, tell Him that honestly. God hears both.

New Words to Know

Grace: Receiving something good that you did not earn and do not deserve. God's grace is the foundation of salvation.

Faith: Trusting in Jesus personally, not just knowing facts about Him. Saving faith includes understanding, agreement, and personal trust.

Repentance: A genuine turning away from sin and toward God. More than feeling sorry, it is a change of direction.

Week 25: What Does Salvation Give Us?

I know salvation saves us from something. But what does it save us for?

After her conversation with her mom, Sophie spent a lot of time thinking.

One evening, she came back with a new question.

'I get that Jesus saves us from sin,' she said. 'But what happens after that? What does being saved actually give you?'

Her mom smiled. 'More than most people realize,' she said. 'You get forgiveness. That means your sin is gone, not just covered over. You get adoption. That means God becomes your Father, not just your Creator. And you get eternal life. Not just life that goes on forever, but a different quality of life that starts now.'

Sophie thought about that. 'So it is not just fire insurance?'

Her mom laughed. 'Not at all. Salvation is not just escaping something bad. It is being brought into something unimaginably good.'

Forgiveness: The Slate Is Clean

The first gift of salvation is forgiveness. Not just that God agrees to tolerate our sin. He removes it.

Psalm 103:12 says, 'As far as the east is from the west, so far has he removed our transgressions from us.'

There is no direction farther than east from west. They never meet. That is how completely God removes forgiven sin. It is not minimized. It is gone.

Justification: Declared Not Guilty

Justification is a legal word. It means being declared righteous before God.

Romans 5:1 says, 'Since we have been justified through faith, we have peace with God through our Lord Jesus Christ.'

Justification is not God pretending we are good. It is God crediting us with Christ's righteousness. The charges are dropped. The verdict is not guilty. And it is permanent.

Adoption: A New Family

One of the most stunning gifts of salvation is adoption into God's family.

John 1:12 says, 'To all who did receive him, to those who believed in his name, he gave the right to become children of God.'

We were separated from God because of sin. Through Jesus, we become His children. God is not just our Creator or our Judge. He is our Father.

Romans 8:15 says we can call out to Him as Abba, the word a child uses for their dad.

Eternal Life: Starting Now

Eternal life does not start only when we die. It starts the moment we trust Jesus.

John 10:10 says, 'I have come that they may have life, and have it to the full.' That full life is available right now.

The new quality of life, knowing God, being free from sin's power, and having hope, begins the moment you are saved. It then continues forever.

Key Verses

"As far as the east is from the west, so far has he removed our transgressions from us." (Psalm 103:12)

"To all who did receive him, to those who believed in his name, he gave the right to become children of God." (John 1:12)

This Week's Verse to Memorize

John 1:12

"To all who did receive him, to those who believed in his name, he gave the right to become children of God."

The word 'right' here means a legal status. God gives it to everyone who receives Jesus. Write this verse out and circle the word 'all.' No one is excluded from this offer.

Activities

Activity 1: Four Gifts

In your journal, draw four gift boxes. Label them: Forgiveness, Justification, Adoption, Eternal Life. Inside each box, write one sentence describing what that gift means in plain language. Then write which gift means the most to you right now and why.

Activity 2: East from West

Read Psalm 103:1-14. List three things David says God does for His people. Then write one sentence about what the east-from-west image tells you about how complete God's forgiveness really is.

Quiz Time

Answer these questions in your journal or workbook:

1. What does justification mean?

2. According to Psalm 103:12, how far has God removed our sin?

3. What does adoption mean in the context of salvation?

4. According to John 1:12, what is given to those who receive Jesus?

5. Does eternal life start only after we die, or does it begin now?

This Week's Challenge

Write a thank-you letter to God in your journal. Thank Him specifically for at least three of the four gifts you learned about this week. Be specific. Name what He has done and why it matters to you personally.

New Words to Know

Forgiveness: God removing our sin completely, not just covering it over. Forgiven sin is gone.

Justification: Being declared righteous by God through faith in Jesus. A legal verdict of not guilty.

Adoption: Being brought into God's family as His child through faith in Jesus.

Eternal Life: The new quality of life that begins when we trust Jesus and continues forever. It starts now, not just after death.

Seven

The Holy Spirit and Christian Life

Weeks 26 through 28

Who is the Holy Spirit? What does He do in us? And what gifts does He give? Three weeks on the person and work of God's Spirit.

Weeks in this unit:

- Week 26: Who Is the Holy Spirit?
- Week 27: What Does the Holy Spirit Do in Us?
- Week 28: Spiritual Gifts

Week 26: Who Is the Holy Spirit?

Is the Holy Spirit a person or just a feeling?

Priya's little brother kept calling the Holy Spirit 'it.'

'The Holy Spirit is not an it,' Priya told him.

'Then what is he?' her brother asked.

Priya thought for a moment. 'He is a person. The third person of the Trinity. He is just as much God as the Father and the Son.'

'But he is invisible,' her brother said.

'So is the wind,' Priya said. 'You cannot see it. But you can feel it. You can see what it does. The Holy Spirit works the same way.'

Her brother considered this. 'So he is real, just not visible?'

'Exactly,' Priya said. 'And he is not far away either. For everyone who trusts Jesus, the Holy Spirit actually lives inside them.'

The Holy Spirit Is a Person

The Holy Spirit is not a feeling or a force. He is a person. He has a mind, emotions, and a will.

First Corinthians 2:10-11 says the Spirit searches the deep things of God. You cannot search something unless you have a mind.

Ephesians 4:30 says the Holy Spirit can be grieved. Only a person can feel grief.

First Corinthians 12:11 says He distributes gifts as He wills. Only a person has a will.

Throughout the Bible, Jesus refers to the Holy Spirit as He, not it. The Spirit is a person, not a power.

The Holy Spirit Is Fully God

The Holy Spirit is not a lesser version of God. He is fully and completely God.

Acts 5:3-4 makes this clear. When Ananias lied to the Holy Spirit, Peter said he had lied to God. Lying to the Spirit is lying to God because the Spirit is God.

The Holy Spirit was present at creation, hovering over the waters in Genesis 1:2. He inspired the writing of Scripture. He raised Jesus from the dead. These are not the actions of a lesser being. They are the actions of God.

How the Spirit Works

The Holy Spirit lives inside every Christian. He makes us aware of sin, draws us to Jesus, and changes us from the inside out.

Jesus called Him the Counselor and the Spirit of truth in John 14:16-17. He is the presence of God with us right now.

The Spirit is not a distant God. He is closer than any friend. He is within every believer, working every day.

Key Verses

"Do not grieve the Holy Spirit of God, with whom you were sealed for the day of redemption." (Ephesians 4:30)

"And I will ask the Father, and he will give you another advocate to help you and be with you forever, the Spirit of truth." (John 14:16-17)

This Week's Verse to Memorize

Ephesians 4:30

"Do not grieve the Holy Spirit of God, with whom you were sealed for the day of redemption."

Only a person can be grieved. This verse proves the Spirit is a person. Write it out and underline the word 'grieve.' What does it tell you about God's care for your choices?

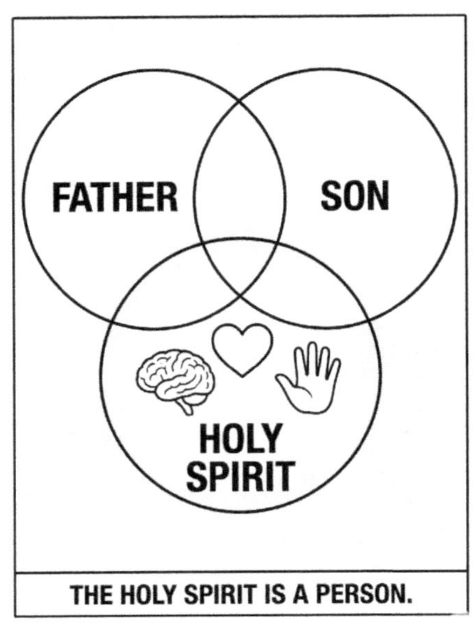

THE HOLY SPIRIT IS A PERSON.

Activities

Activity 1: Person, Not a Force

In your journal, write down the three qualities that make someone a person: having a mind, having emotions, and having a will. For each one, write the Bible verse from this week that shows the Holy Spirit has that quality. Then write one sentence explaining why it matters that the Spirit is a person and not just a force.

Activity 2: Wind Comparison

Read John 3:8, where Jesus compares the Spirit to wind. Write down two ways the Holy Spirit is like wind based on that verse and what you learned this week. Then write one way the comparison breaks down, where the Spirit is different from the wind.

Quiz Time

Answer these questions in your journal or workbook:

1. What three qualities show that the Holy Spirit is a person?

2. According to Acts 5:3-4, what does lying to the Holy Spirit equal?

3. Where was the Holy Spirit present in Genesis 1:2?

4. What names does Jesus use for the Holy Spirit in John 14:16-17?

5. Where does the Holy Spirit live for every believer?

This Week's Challenge

This week, start each morning by acknowledging the Holy Spirit. Before you get out of bed, say a simple prayer: 'Holy Spirit, You are with me today. Help me to listen to You.' Do this every day and write down at the end of the week whether it changed how your days felt.

New Words to Know

Holy Spirit: The third person of the Trinity. Fully God, fully personal, present within every believer.

Counselor: One of the names Jesus uses for the Holy Spirit in John 14. It means one who comes alongside to help.

Grieve: To cause sorrow or sadness. The Bible says we can grieve the Holy Spirit by our sin. This shows He is a person with emotions.

Week 27: What Does the Holy Spirit Do in Us?

How does the Holy Spirit actually change a person?

Marcus was trying to stop losing his temper.

He had been trying for months. He would do well for a few days, then something would set him off and he would be right back where he started.

'I keep failing,' he told his dad. 'I do not think I can change.'

'You are right that you cannot change yourself,' his dad said. 'Not on your own. But that is not how God designed it to work.'

'What do you mean?' Marcus asked.

'The Holy Spirit does not stand outside you cheering, you on. He lives inside you. He is the one doing the changing. Your job is to stay close to Him, not to fix yourself by trying harder.'

Marcus looked up. 'So it is not all on me?'

'You still make choices,' his dad said. 'But the power to change comes from Him, not from you.'

Conviction: Showing Us the Problem

The Holy Spirit is the one who makes us aware of sin. John 16:8 says He will convict the world of sin, righteousness, and judgment.

That feeling you get when you know you have done something wrong? That is the Spirit working. He does not convict us to crush us. He convicts us so we will turn to God and find forgiveness.

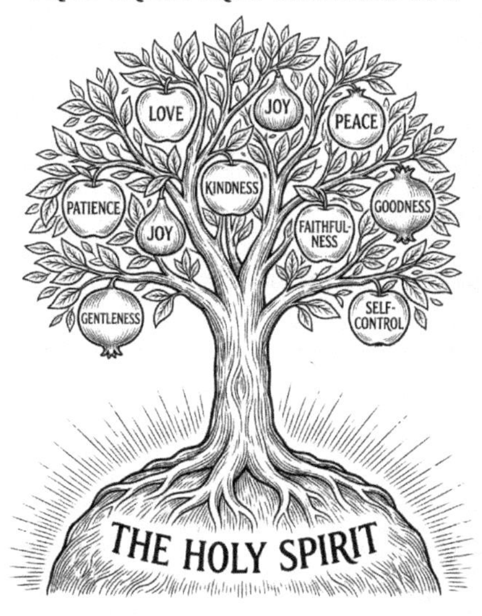

Regeneration: Making Us New

Before a person trusts Jesus, they are spiritually dead. The Holy Spirit is the one who makes new life possible.

Jesus said in John 3:5-6 that no one can enter God's kingdom without being born of the Spirit.

This new birth is called regeneration. It is not something we do. It is something the Spirit does in us when we turn to God.

Sanctification: Making Us More Like Jesus

After we are saved, the Spirit begins the lifelong process of making us more like Jesus. This is called sanctification.

Galatians 5:22-23 describes the fruit of the Spirit: love, joy, peace, patience, kindness, goodness, faithfulness, gentleness, and self-control. These are not things we manufacture. They grow when the Spirit is working in us.

We still make choices. We still fail. But the Spirit keeps working, keeps convicting, keeps restoring, and keeps growing us.

Indwelling: God Is Always with You

First Corinthians 6:19 says your body is a temple of the Holy Spirit. God does not live in a building anymore. He lives in people.

This means you are never alone. You never face a hard moment without God present. The same Spirit who raised Jesus from the dead lives in you.

Key Verses

"But the fruit of the Spirit is love, joy, peace, forbearance, kindness, goodness, faithfulness, gentleness and self-control." (Galatians 5:22-23)

"Do you not know that your bodies are temples of the Holy Spirit, who is in you, whom you have received from God?" (1 Corinthians 6:19)

This Week's Verse to Memorize

Galatians 5:22-23

"The fruit of the Spirit is love, joy, peace, forbearance, kindness, goodness, faithfulness, gentleness and self-control."

These nine qualities are called fruit because they grow naturally from a healthy connection to the Spirit. Write each one out and then circle the two you most want to grow in right now.

Activities

Activity 1: Four Works of the Spirit

In your journal, draw four boxes and label them: Conviction, Regeneration, Sanctification, Indwelling. Write a one-sentence description of each in your own words. Then write one sentence about how each one shows that the Spirit's work is personal, not just general.

Activity 2: Fruit Inventory

Look at the nine fruits of the Spirit in Galatians 5:22-23. Honestly rate yourself on each one from 1 to 5. Which are strongest in you right now? Which needs the most growth? Write a short prayer asking the Spirit to grow the weakest fruit in your life.

Quiz Time

Answer these questions in your journal or workbook:

1. What does it mean that the Holy Spirit convicts us?

2. What is regeneration?

3. What is sanctification?

4. Name five of the nine fruits of the Spirit from Galatians 5:22-23.

5. According to 1 Corinthians 6:19, what is your body?

This Week's Challenge

Pick one fruit of the Spirit you want to grow in this week. Write it at the top of a page in your journal. Every evening, write one sentence about how you either showed that quality or missed it that day. At the end of the week, look back at what you wrote. What do you notice?

New Words to Know

Conviction: The Holy Spirit's work of making us aware of sin so that we turn to God for forgiveness.

Regeneration: The new birth. The Spirit's work of making a spiritually dead person alive to God.

Sanctification: The ongoing work of the Holy Spirit, making believers more like Jesus over their lifetime.

Indwelling: The Holy Spirit living permanently inside every believer from the moment of salvation.

Week 28: Spiritual Gifts

Does God really give every believer a spiritual gift?

Zoe did not think she had any gifts.

Her friend could sing beautifully. Her cousin was a gifted teacher. Everyone around her seemed to have something obvious and impressive.

'I am not good at anything spiritual,' she told her youth pastor.

He smiled. 'That is not how gifts work,' he said. 'Spiritual gifts are not about being impressive. They are given by the Spirit to help the church. Some gifts are quiet. Some are practical. Some are relational. But every believer has at least one.'

'How do I find mine?' Zoe asked.

'Serve,' he said. 'Try things. Pay attention to what helps people. Ask others what they see in you. Gifts often show up before we recognize them ourselves.'

What Are Spiritual Gifts?

Spiritual gifts are abilities the Holy Spirit gives to believers for the purpose of building up the church and serving others.

First Corinthians 12:7 says, 'To each one the manifestation of the Spirit is given for the common good.' The key phrase is for the common good. Gifts are not given to make you look impressive. They are given to help other people.

First Corinthians 12, Romans 12, and Ephesians 4 all list spiritual gifts. Together they include teaching, encouragement, serving, giving, leadership, mercy, faith, and hospitality, among others.

Every Believer Has at Least One

First Corinthians 12:11 says the Spirit gives gifts to each one as He wills. No one is left out. Every believer receives at least one gift.

This means no Christian is spiritually useless. You have something the body of Christ needs. Your gift may be quiet or visible, behind the scenes or upfront. But it is real and it is needed.

Gifts Are for Others, Not Just Yourself

First Peter 4:10 says, 'Each of you should use whatever gift you have received to serve others, as faithful stewards of God's grace in its various forms.'

Gifts are meant to flow outward. The whole point is to serve the people around you.

How to Discover Your Gifts

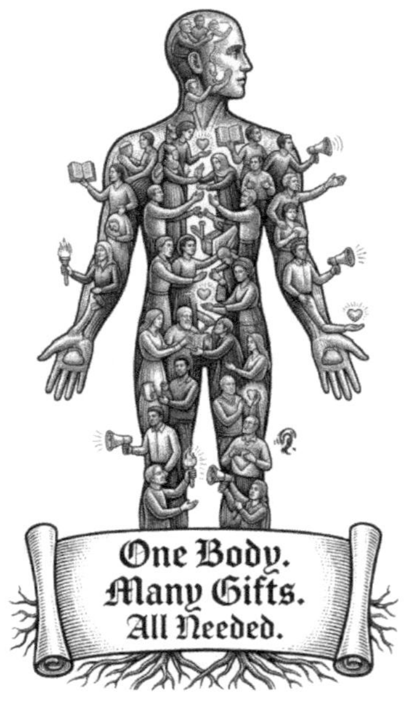

The best way to find your gifts is to start serving and pay attention. Try teaching a younger child. Help with a practical need. Encourage someone who is struggling.

When your gift connects with a need, you will often feel it. Others will confirm it. And the church will be better for it.

Key Verses

"To each one the manifestation of the Spirit is given for the common good." (1 Corinthians 12:7)

"Each of you should use whatever gift you have received to serve others, as faithful stewards of God's grace in its various forms." (1 Peter 4:10)

This Week's Verse to Memorize

1 Corinthians 12:7

"To each one the manifestation of the Spirit is given for the common good."

Notice two things: 'each one' means everyone gets a gift. 'Common good' means it is for others. Write this verse out and put a box around both phrases.

Activities

Activity 1: Gift Survey

Read Romans 12:6-8 and 1 Corinthians 12:8-10. List every gift mentioned. Then circle three that you think might describe you. Ask one parent or trusted adult if they agree, and write down what they say.

Activity 2: Gift in Action

Choose one gift from the list and do one act of service this week that uses it. If you think your gift might be encouragement, write a note to someone who needs it. If it might be serving, help with a practical task without being asked. Then write in your journal about how it felt.

Quiz Time

Answer these questions in your journal or workbook:

1. What is a spiritual gift?

2. According to 1 Corinthians 12:7, why does the Spirit give gifts?

3. Does every believer receive a spiritual gift?

4. Name three spiritual gifts mentioned in the Bible.

5. According to 1 Peter 4:10, how should we use our gifts?

This Week's Challenge

This week, do one thing to serve your church or family using a gift you think you might have. Do not wait until you are sure. Just serve. Then ask someone who saw you in action what they noticed. Their feedback is one of the best ways to confirm a gift.

New Words to Know

Spiritual Gift: An ability given by the Holy Spirit to a believer for the purpose of serving others and building up the church.

Body of Christ: A biblical picture of the church as a human body, where every member is a different part with a different function, all needed.

Steward: Someone who manages something that belongs to someone else. We are stewards of our spiritual gifts because they come from God.

Eight

Prayer and Worship

Weeks 29 through 31

What is prayer? How do we pray? And what does worship really mean? Three weeks on talking to God and living for Him.

Weeks in this unit:

- Week 29: What Is Prayer?
- Week 30: How Do We Pray?
- Week 31: What Is Worship?

Week 29: What Is Prayer?

Why should I pray if God already knows everything?

Jaylen had not prayed in weeks.

He wanted to. But every time he sat down to try, he did not know what to say. It felt like leaving a voicemail for someone who might not pick up.

He told his grandma about it.

'Does God actually hear me?' he asked.

'He does,' she said. 'Prayer is not a performance. It is a conversation. You would not worry about finding the perfect words with me, would you?'

'No,' Jaylen said.

'Talk to God the same way. Tell him what is actually on your mind. He already knows anyway. The point is not to inform Him. The point is to be with Him.'

Prayer Is a Conversation, Not a Performance

Prayer is simply talking to God. It is not about having the right words, the right posture, or the right length.

First Thessalonians 5:17 says to pray continually. That does not mean you never stop talking. It means you keep the conversation going throughout your day. A quick thank you. A moment of asking for help. An honest expression of how you feel.

God invites this. He does not want formal speeches. He wants a real relationship.

The Four Main Types of Prayer

The Bible shows us several kinds of prayer. Each one reflects a different part of our relationship with God.

Praise: Telling God who He is and how great He is.

Thanksgiving: Thanking God for what He has done. Philippians 4:6 says to bring requests to God with thanksgiving.

Confession: Being honest about sin and asking for forgiveness. First John 1:9 says if we confess our sins, He is faithful to forgive.

Supplication: Asking God for things, both for yourself and for others. Praying for others is called intercession.

Prayer is a conversation, not a performance

Does God Always Answer?

Yes. But not always in the way we expect.

Sometimes God says yes. Sometimes he says not yet. Sometimes He says no, because He can see what we cannot.

James 4:3 warns that we can ask with wrong motives. God answers prayer according to His wisdom and love, not our preferences. The goal of prayer is not to get what we want. It is to stay connected to the God who always knows what is best.

Key Verses

"Do not be anxious about anything, but in every situation, by prayer and petition, with thanksgiving, present your requests to God." (Philippians 4:6)

"Pray continually." (1 Thessalonians 5:17)

This Week's Verse to Memorize

Philippians 4:6

"Do not be anxious about anything, but in every situation, by prayer and petition, with thanksgiving, present your requests to God."

This verse connects anxiety and prayer directly. Whatever makes you anxious this week, bring it to God in prayer. Write it out and then write one thing you are currently anxious about that you want to hand over to Him.

Activities

Activity 1: Four Types of Prayer

Write a short prayer using all four types: Praise, Thanksgiving, Confession, and Supplication. Label each section. Keep each part to two or three sentences. This will probably be one of the most complete prayers you have ever written.

Activity 2: Prayer Journal

Start a simple prayer log this week. Each day, write down one thing you prayed for and leave a space next to it. Over the coming weeks, return to this log and write what happened. Watching God answer over time is one of the most faith-building things you can do.

Quiz Time

Answer these questions in your journal or workbook:

1. What is prayer in the simplest definition?

2. Name the four types of prayer from this week.

3. What does 'intercession' mean?

4. Does God always answer prayer? What are three ways He might answer?

5. According to 1 Thessalonians 5:17, how often should we pray?

This Week's Challenge

Set a simple goal this week: pray every day. It does not need to be long. Even two minutes counts. At the end of the week, write about what was hardest about keeping that habit and what surprised you about it.

New Words to Know

Prayer: Talking to God. It includes praise, thanksgiving, confession, and requests.

Intercession: Praying on behalf of someone else. When you ask God to help another person, you are interceding for them.

Supplication: A humble request brought to God. One of the four main types of prayer.

Confession: Being honest with God about sin and asking for forgiveness.

Week: 30: How Do We Pray?

Is there a right way and a wrong way to pray?

Ella had read the Lord's Prayer a hundred times.

She could say it from memory. She said it at church every week.

But one day her teacher asked, 'Do you know why Jesus taught this prayer?'

Ella thought about it. 'So we would have the right words?'

'Not exactly,' her teacher said. 'Jesus gave it as a model, not a script. He was showing His disciples the shape of a good prayer, not the exact words to repeat every time.'

'So we are not supposed to say it word for word?' Ella asked.

'You can,' her teacher said. 'But the deeper idea is to let it teach you what prayer should include. Start with God. Ask for His kingdom. Then bring your needs. Then deal with forgiveness. That is the shape of a healthy prayer life.'

The Lord's Prayer as a Model

In Matthew 6:9-13, Jesus teaches His disciples how to pray. He does not say recite this prayer. He says pray like this.

The Lord's Prayer is a template. It shows us what a complete, healthy prayer looks like.

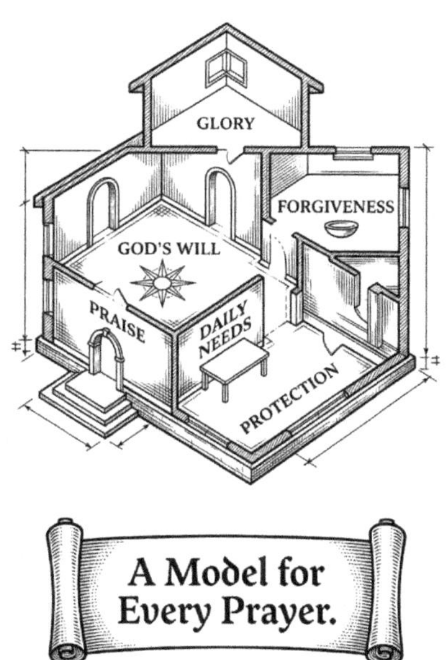

Six Parts of the Lord's Prayer

- Our Father in heaven, hallowed be your name. Start with God. Acknowledge who He is before you bring your list.
- Your kingdom come, your will be done on earth as in heaven. Before asking for what you want, ask for what God wants.
- Give us today our daily bread. Bring your real needs. God cares about practical things.
- Forgive us our debts, as we also have forgiven our debtors. Prayer includes confession and forgiving others. These go together.
- Lead us not into temptation, but deliver us from evil. Ask for protection and help to resist sin.
- For yours is the kingdom, the power, and the glory forever. Prayer begins and ends with who God is.

Persistence and Honesty in Prayer

Jesus told a parable in Luke 18:1-8 about a widow who kept coming to a judge with her request. He told this story to show that we should keep praying and not give up.

This does not mean God needs to be pestered. It means persistent prayer keeps our hearts connected to God as we wait for His answer.

Be honest when you pray. David cried out to God in the Psalms. He expressed anger, grief, doubt, and fear. God did not reject those prayers. He welcomed them. Honest prayer is better than polished prayer.

Key Verses

"This, then, is how you should pray: Our Father in heaven, hallowed be your name, your kingdom come, your will be done, on earth as it is in heaven." (Matthew 6:9-10)

"Then Jesus told his disciples a parable to show them that they should always pray and not give up." (Luke 18:1)

This Week's Verse to Memorize

Matthew 6:9-10

"Our Father in heaven, hallowed be your name, your kingdom come, your will be done, on earth as it is in heaven."

The first thing Jesus teaches us to pray is for God's will, not our own. Write this verse and then write one sentence about what it means to pray for God's will before you ask for what you want.

Activities

Activity 1: Pray Through the Model

Use the six parts of the Lord's Prayer as a guide and write your own personal prayer. Do not use the exact words of the Lord's Prayer. Instead, fill each section with your own words and your own situation. This is exactly what Jesus intended when He said 'pray like this.'

Activity 2: Honest Prayer

Read Psalm 22:1-11. This is one of David's most honest and raw prayers. Write down three emotions David expresses to God. Then write a short prayer of your own that is just as honest. Tell God exactly how you feel about something, without dressing it up.

Quiz Time

Answer these questions in your journal or workbook:

1. Did Jesus give the Lord's Prayer as a script to repeat or as a model to follow?

2. What is the first thing the Lord's Prayer focuses on?

3. What does it mean to pray for daily bread?

4. What is the point of the parable Jesus tells in Luke 18:1-8?

5. Why is honest prayer better than polished prayer?

This Week's Challenge

This week, pray through the Lord's Prayer in your own words every day. Do not recite it. Rewrite each section in your own words each morning. By the end of the week you will have written seven personal prayers, and you will know the shape of the Lord's Prayer in a new way.

New Words to Know

The Lord's Prayer: The model prayer Jesus taught His disciples in Matthew 6:9-13. It is a template for all prayer, not a script to be repeated mechanically.

Persistence in Prayer: Continuing to bring requests to God over time, trusting that He hears and will answer in His timing.

Lament: A type of prayer that expresses grief, pain, or confusion honestly to God. The Psalms are full of lament. God welcomes this kind of prayer.

Week 31: What Is Worship?

Is worship just singing? Or is it something bigger?

Rosa thought worship only happened on Sunday morning.

Then her youth leader said something that surprised her.

'You can worship while you wash the dishes,' she said.

Rosa looked skeptical.

'Worship is not a style of music or a time slot,' her leader explained. 'It is an orientation. It is living in a way that says: God, you matter most. You can do that anywhere. In any task. At any moment.'

Rosa thought about her soccer game that week. She had played selfishly, trying to score instead of passing to open teammates.

'So not playing selfishly would be worship?' she asked.

'Playing for the glory of God instead of your own glory? Absolutely,' her leader said. 'That is worship.'

Worship Is More Than Music

Most people think worship is the singing part of a church service. But that is only one small piece of it.

Romans 12:1 says, 'Offer your bodies as a living sacrifice, holy and pleasing to God. This is your true and proper worship.' A living sacrifice is not a song. It is a life.

Worship is anything you do that says God is most important. It happens when you are honest because He is true. When you are kind because He is love. When you work hard because He made you for a purpose. All of it is worship when done for Him.

Corporate Worship: Why We Meet Together

Meeting with other believers to worship together matters. Hebrews 10:25 says do not give up meeting together, as some are in the habit of doing.

When we gather, we sing, hear God's Word, pray together, take communion, and encourage each other. These are not just traditions. They are ways of reminding each other who God is and what He has done.

Corporate worship does something that private worship cannot fully do on its own. It connects you to the wider family of God.

Making All of Life Worship

First Corinthians 10:31 says whatever you do, do it all for the glory of God. We saw this in Unit 4. It applies here, too.

Doing your homework carefully can be worship. Treating a sibling with kindness can be worship. Playing a sport with integrity can be worship.

The question is not: am I in church? The question is: am I living for God? When the answer is yes, your whole life becomes an act of worship.

Key Verses

"Therefore, I urge you, brothers and sisters, in view of God's mercy, to offer your bodies as a living sacrifice, holy and pleasing to God. This is your true and proper worship." (Romans 12:1)

"And let us not give up meeting together, as some are in the habit of doing, but encouraging one another." (Hebrews 10:25)

This Week's Verse to Memorize

Romans 12:1

"Offer your bodies as a living sacrifice, holy and pleasing to God. This is your true and proper worship."

A living sacrifice is not something you do once. It is something you choose every day. Write this verse out and then write one specific way you could offer yourself as a living sacrifice tomorrow.

Activities

Activity 1: Worship Audit

Think about your typical Tuesday. List ten things you do on a normal school day. For each one, write yes or no: could this be an act of worship? Then write one sentence about what would need to change in your heart or behavior for each one to become worship.

Activity 2: Corporate Worship Reflection

Think about the last time you were at a church service or worship gathering. Write down three things that happened and what each one was meant to do. For example: we sang together to remind ourselves who God is. Then write one thing you could do to engage more intentionally next time.

Quiz Time

Answer these questions in your journal or workbook:

1. According to Romans 12:1, what is our true and proper worship?

2. Is worship limited to singing? What else can it include?

3. Why does Hebrews 10:25 say we should not give up meeting together?

4. What is the difference between corporate worship and private worship?

5. Name one ordinary activity from your daily life that could be an act of worship.

This Week's Challenge

Choose one ordinary task you do every day this week, like making your bed, doing homework, or eating dinner. Before you do it each day, say quietly: 'God, I want to do this for you.' Notice whether it changes how you approach the task. Write about what you noticed at the end of the week.

New Words to Know

Worship: Anything done in a way that honors God and says He is most important. It includes singing, prayer, and all of daily life.

Corporate Worship: Worshipping together as a community of believers. Sunday gatherings are the primary example.

Living Sacrifice: The phrase Paul uses in Romans 12:1 to describe a life fully given to God. Unlike an animal sacrifice, a living sacrifice keeps on giving every day.

Sacred and Secular: Two categories people often use to separate church life from regular life. The Bible teaches that this division is false. All of life belongs to God.

Nine

The Church

Weeks 32 through 34

What is the Church? Why does it matter? And what are baptism and communion all about? Three weeks on the community Jesus is building.

Weeks in this unit:

- Week 32: What Is the Church?
- Week 33: Why Does the Church Matter?
- Week 34: What Is Communion and Baptism?

Week 32: What Is the Church?

Is church a building, an event, or something else entirely?

Nadia had never really thought about what the word church meant.

She went every Sunday. She knew the building. She knew the people.

But one week, her family's church met in a park because the building was being repaired. And it felt exactly the same.

'Why does it feel like church even without the building?' she asked her dad on the way home.

'Because the church is not the building,' her dad said. 'The church is the people. Wherever believers gather in Jesus's name, that is the church.'

'So the church is us?' Nadia asked.

'Exactly,' her dad said. 'The building is just a tool. The people are the point.'

The Church Is People, Not a Place

The word church comes from the Greek word ekklesia, which means a called-out assembly. It refers to a group of people called together, not a structure made of bricks and mortar.

When Jesus says in Matthew 16:18 that He will build His church, He is not talking about a building project. He is talking about gathering people who belong to Him.

First Corinthians 3:16 says you are God's temple. Not the building you meet in. You. The people of God together are where God dwells on earth now.

The Universal Church and the Local Church

The Bible uses the word church in two ways.

The universal church includes every believer who has ever lived, across every time and place. If you trust in Jesus, you are part of this church, whether you have ever attended a service or not.

The local church is a specific group of believers who meet together regularly in a particular place. This is where the universal church becomes visible and practical in your everyday life.

Both matter. But the local church is where you actually live out your faith with real people.

The Body of Christ

First Corinthians 12:27 says, 'Now you are the body of Christ, and each one of you is a part of it.'

The church is not a club or an organization. It is a living body with Jesus as its head. (Colossians 1:18.) Every member has a role. No part is unimportant.

This means the church needs you. Not just your attendance. Your gifts, your presence, your service. A body with missing parts does not function as well as it should.

Key Verses

"And I tell you that you are Peter, and on this rock I will build my church, and the gates of Hades will not overcome it." (Matthew 16:18)

"Now you are the body of Christ, and each one of you is a part of it." (1 Corinthians 12:27)

This Week's Verse to Memorize

1 Corinthians 12:27

"Now you are the body of Christ, and each one of you is a part of it."

The word 'each one' means you personally have a part to play. Write this verse out and then write one sentence describing what part of the body you think you might be and why.

Activities

Activity 1: Universal and Local

In your journal, draw two overlapping circles. Label one Universal Church and the other Local Church. In the universal circle, write three characteristics of the whole body of all believers. In the local circle, write three things your specific church does that make it the universal church made visible. In the overlapping section, write what both have in common.

Activity 2: Body Parts

Read 1 Corinthians 12:12-26. Paul compares the church to a human body. Write down three specific points he makes about how body parts relate to each other. Then write one sentence about how each point applies to your church community specifically.

Quiz Time

Answer these questions in your journal or workbook:

1. What does the Greek word ekklesia mean?

2. What is the difference between the universal church and the local church?

3. According to 1 Corinthians 3:16, where does God dwell now?

4. Who is the head of the church according to Colossians 1:18?

5. Why does the church need every member, not just the leaders?

This Week's Challenge

This week, thank one person in your church for something specific they do. Not a general compliment. Something specific: the way they greet people, the way they serve, the way they teach. Recognizing others' parts in the body is itself an act of being part of the body.

New Words to Know

Ekklesia: The Greek word translated as church. It means a called-out assembly of people, not a building.

Universal Church: All believers everywhere across all time who belong to Jesus Christ.

Local Church: A specific community of believers in a particular place who meet together regularly.

Body of Christ: A biblical picture of the church as a living body with Jesus as its head and every believer as a necessary part.

Week 33: Why Does the Church Matter?

Can I follow Jesus without being part of a church?

Eli had stopped going to Youth Group.

It was not that he stopped believing. He still prayed. He still read his Bible sometimes. He just did not see why he needed other people to do it.

His older sister listened and then asked him a question.

'Have you ever tried to do a group project by yourself?'

'Yes,' Eli said. 'It is terrible.'

'Faith is a little like that,' she said. 'You can believe on your own. But God designed it to be done together. You need people who will encourage you when you are struggling, correct you when you are wrong, and remind you of what is true when you forget. That is what the church is for.'

Eli thought about the last few months. He had been struggling more than usual. And he had been doing it completely alone.

Community: You Were Not Meant to Go It Alone

God designed human beings for community. This was true before sin entered the world, and it is still true now.

The early church in Acts 2:42-47 devoted itself to teaching, fellowship, breaking bread, and prayer. They met daily. They shared what they had. And God added to their number every day.

This is not a picture of people reluctantly attending an obligation. It is a picture of people who genuinely needed and wanted each other.

Accountability: We Help Each Other Stay on Track

Hebrews 3:13 says to encourage one another daily, so that none of you may be hardened by sin's deceitfulness.

Sin is deceptive. It convinces you that you are fine when you are not. Other believers who know you well can see what you cannot always see about yourself.

This is not about judgment. It is about honest friendship. The church is meant to be a place where people help each other stay true to what they believe.

Mission: The Church Exists for the World

Jesus gave His followers a clear assignment in Matthew 28:19-20. Go and make disciples of all nations.

The church does not exist only for the people already inside it. It exists to reach people who are not yet part of it.

Every local church is meant to be an outpost of God's kingdom in its neighborhood. Serving, welcoming, sharing the gospel, and showing the world what it looks like when people live under Jesus's rule.

You are part of that mission right now, not just when you grow up.

Key Verses

"They devoted themselves to the apostles' teaching and to fellowship, to the breaking of bread and to prayer." (Acts 2:42)

"Therefore go and make disciples of all nations, baptizing them in the name of the Father and of the Son and of the Holy Spirit." (Matthew 28:19)

This Week's Verse to Memorize

Matthew 28:19

"Therefore go and make disciples of all nations, baptizing them in the name of the Father and of the Son and of the Holy Spirit."

This is called the Great Commission. It is Jesus's final instruction before He ascended. Write it out and circle the word 'go.' The church does not wait for the world to come to it.

Activities

Activity 1: Acts 2 Church

Read Acts 2:42-47. List every activity the early church did together. Then write next to each one whether your own church does something similar. Which ones are present? Which ones are missing? What would it look like to have all of them?

Activity 2: Your Part in the Mission

The Great Commission applies to every believer, including you. Write down two specific ways someone your age could participate in the church's mission right now, not someday. Think about your school, your neighborhood, and your friendships.

Quiz Time

Answer these questions in your journal or workbook:

1. Name three things the early church in Acts 2 devoted themselves to.

2. What does Hebrews 3:13 say we should do for each other daily?

3. Why does Hebrews 3:13 say sin is dangerous?

4. What is the Great Commission?

5. Does the church's mission only apply to adults? Explain.

This Week's Challenge

This week, do one thing for someone outside your church community. It can be small: a kind word, a helpful action, an invitation. Then write about it in your journal. Reaching outward is practicing the mission even at a small scale.

New Words to Know

Fellowship: Genuine, shared life among believers. More than socializing, it involves mutual care, honesty, and support.

Accountability: The practice of allowing other believers to speak honestly into your life and help you stay faithful.

Great Commission: Jesus's command in Matthew 28:19-20 for His followers to go and make disciples of all nations.

Mission: The church's God-given purpose to reach the world with the gospel and make disciples.

Week 34: What Is Communion and Baptism?

Why does Jesus want us to keep doing these two specific things?

At his church, Daniel had watched people get baptized many times.

He had also taken communion every month.

But he had never really understood what either one meant.

'Are these just traditions?' he asked his pastor after a service.

'They are much more than traditions,' his pastor said. 'Jesus gave His followers two specific practices to keep doing until He returns. Baptism and communion. They are not just rituals. They are physical pictures of spiritual realities.'

'What do they picture?' Daniel asked.

'Baptism pictures what happened when you were saved. Death to your old life and rising to a new one. Communion pictures what Jesus did on the cross and reminds you that His body was broken and His blood was shed for you.'

'So every time we do them, we are telling the same story?' Daniel asked.

'Exactly,' his pastor said. 'The gospel in physical form.'

What Are the Ordinances?

Jesus gave the church two practices to observe. Most Protestant churches call them ordinances, meaning they were commanded by Jesus. Some churches call them sacraments.

Both baptism and communion point to the gospel. They do not save you. But they tell the story of salvation in a physical, visible way.

Baptism: Going Public

Baptism is the act of being immersed in or sprinkled with water as a public declaration of faith in Jesus.

Matthew 28:19 includes baptism in the Great Commission. Acts 2:41 says those who accepted Peter's message were baptized.

Baptism does not save a person. Salvation happens through faith alone. But baptism is the normal first step of obedience after trusting Jesus. It says publicly: I belong to Him.

Symbolically, going under the water pictures dying to the old life. Coming back up pictures rising to new life in Christ. Romans 6:4 describes it this way.

Communion: Remembering the Cross

Communion, also called the Lord's Supper or the Eucharist, is the regular practice of eating bread and drinking from a cup together as a church.

Jesus established it at the Last Supper in Luke 22:19-20. He told His disciples to do this in remembrance of Him.

The bread represents His body, broken for us. The cup represents His blood, poured out for the forgiveness of sins. Every time believers take communion, they are proclaiming the Lord's death until He comes back. (1 Corinthians 11:26.)

Communion is not just a memorial. It is a declaration. The gospel, enacted together, every time.

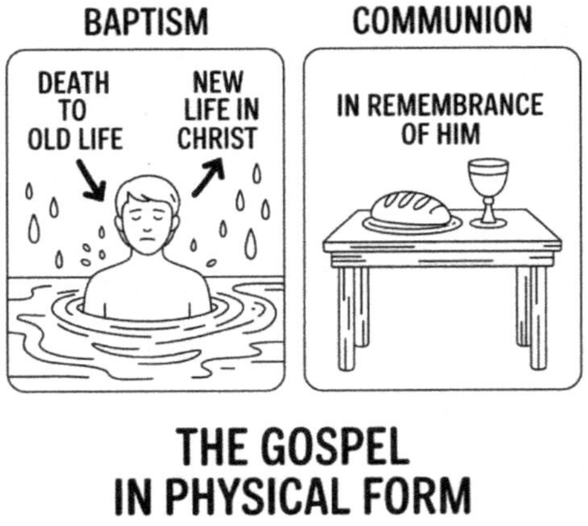

Key Verses

"We were therefore buried with him through baptism into death in order that, just as Christ was raised from the dead through the glory of the Father, we too may live a new life." (Romans 6:4)

"For whenever you eat this bread and drink this cup, you proclaim the Lord's death until he comes." (1 Corinthians 11:26)

This Week's Verse to Memorize

1 Corinthians 11:26

"For whenever you eat this bread and drink this cup, you proclaim the Lord's death until he comes."

Every communion is a proclamation. You are announcing something true about Jesus to everyone present. Write this verse out and then write one sentence about what it means to proclaim something without words.

Activities

Activity 1: What Each One Means

In your journal, draw a simple two-column chart. Label one column Baptism and the other Communion. For each one, write: what it is, what it pictures, and what it does not do. Use what you learned this week and the Bible verses provided.

Activity 2: Gospel in Physical Form

Both ordinances tell the story of the gospel physically. Write out the gospel story from Unit 6 in four sentences. Then next to each sentence, write which part of baptism or communion connects to that part of the story.

Quiz Time

Answer these questions in your journal or workbook:

1. What is the difference between the terms 'ordinance' and 'sacrament'?

2. Does baptism save a person? Explain.

3. What does baptism symbolize according to Romans 6:4?

4. What do the bread and cup represent in communion?

5. According to 1 Corinthians 11:26, what are believers doing every time they take communion?

This Week's Challenge

If you have been baptized, write in your journal about what it meant to you and what you were declaring. If you have not yet been baptized but have trusted Jesus, talk with a parent or pastor this week about what baptism would mean for you. If you are still thinking through faith, write down your questions honestly.

New Words to Know

Ordinance: A practice commanded by Jesus for the church to observe. Baptism and communion are the two ordinances.

Sacrament: Another word some churches use for ordinance. The word suggests that God works through the practice in a special way.

Baptism: A public act of going into and coming out of water as a declaration of faith in Jesus and identification with His death and resurrection.

Communion: The regular practice of eating bread and drinking from a cup together as a church, in remembrance of Jesus's death and in proclamation of His return.

Ten

Angels, Spritual Warfare, and the Unseen World

Weeks 35 through 37

Weeks in this unit:

- Week 35: What Are Angels?
- Week 36: What Is the Devil and Where Did He Come From?
- Week 37: What Is Spiritual Warfare?

Week 35: What Are Angels?

Are angels real? And what are they actually like?

Priya's younger sister had just started asking about angels.

She wanted to know if they had wings. If they looked like people. If she had one following her around right now.

Priya had grown up hearing about angels but realized she had never looked at what the Bible actually said about them.

So she and her sister sat down and started reading together.

'They are not what I thought,' Priya said after a while.

'What do you mean?' her sister asked.

'They are not chubby babies with harps. They are powerful messengers who serve God. And when people in the Bible actually saw one, their first reaction was usually to fall on their face in fear.'

Her sister's eyes went wide. 'Really?'

'Every time one shows up in the Bible and says something,' Priya said, 'the first words are almost always: do not be afraid.'

Angels Are Created Beings

Angels are real. The Bible mentions them hundreds of times. But they are not gods or mini-gods. They are created beings, just like humans, though different in nature and ability.

Psalm 148:2-5 calls angels to praise God and notes that God created them. Colossians 1:16 says all things were created by Jesus, including things in the heavenly realms. Angels are part of that creation.

Because they are created, angels are not all-knowing, not all-powerful, and not everywhere at once. Only God has those qualities.

What Angels Do

Angels serve God and carry out His purposes. The Bible shows them doing several things.

They deliver messages. The word angel comes from a Greek word meaning messenger. Gabriel appeared to Mary in Luke 1:26-28 to announce the birth of Jesus.

They worship God. Revelation 4 and 5 picture angels continuously worshipping before God's throne.

They serve believers. Hebrews 1:14 calls them ministering spirits sent to serve those who will inherit salvation.

They carry out God's judgments. In Acts 12:23, an angel strikes down a king who accepted worship meant for God alone.

Angels Are Not to Be Worshipped

One of the clearest biblical warnings about angels is that they must not be worshipped.

When the apostle John fell at an angel's feet in Revelation 22:8-9, the angel immediately stopped him. He said: do not do it. I am a fellow servant. Worship God.

Angels point to God. They do not receive worship meant for Him. However impressive they are, they are servants, not the One being served.

Key Verses

"Are not all angels ministering spirits sent to serve those who will inherit salvation?" (Hebrews 1:14)

"Do not do it! I am a fellow servant with you... Worship God!" (Revelation 22:9)

This Week's Verse to Memorize

Hebrews 1:14

"Are not all angels ministering spirits sent to serve those who will inherit salvation?"

This verse shows that angels serve believers, not the other way around. Write it out and then write one sentence about what it means that powerful beings like angels are sent to serve you.

Activities

Activity 1: Angel Appearances in the Bible

Look up three of these angel appearances and write a two-sentence summary of each: Luke 1:26-38, Matthew 28:2-7, Acts 5:17-20. For each one, write what the angel did and how the people responded. What patterns do you notice?

Activity 2: What Angels Are Not

Based on what you learned this week, write a short paragraph correcting three common misconceptions people have about angels. For each misconception, write what the Bible actually says instead.

Quiz Time

Answer these questions in your journal or workbook:

1. Are angels created beings or eternal beings like God?

2. What does the word 'angel' mean?

3. Name two things angels do according to the Bible.

4. What did the angel say when John tried to worship him in Revelation 22?

5. According to Hebrews 1:14, what is the role of angels toward believers?

DO NOT BE AFRAID.

This Week's Challenge

This week, read Psalm 91 slowly. It is one of the Bible's most vivid passages about God's protection, including the role of angels. Write down two promises from that psalm that stood out to you and explain why.

New Words to Know

Angel: A created spiritual being who serves God. The word means messenger in Greek.

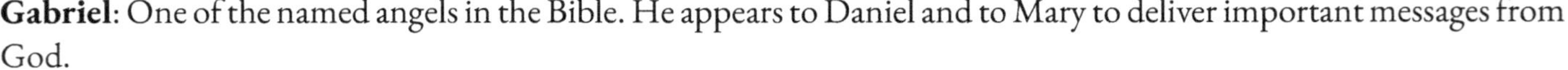

Gabriel: One of the named angels in the Bible. He appears to Daniel and to Mary to deliver important messages from God.

Ministering Spirits: The phrase Hebrews 1:14 uses for angels. It means servants sent on behalf of God to care for His people.

Heavenly Realms: The spiritual dimension of reality where angels, demons, and God's throne exist, alongside the physical world we see.

WeeK 36: What Is the Devil and Where Did He Come From?

Is Satan real? And how much power does he actually have?

'Is the devil real?' Marco asked his dad one evening.

He had heard people talk about Satan at church, but was not sure whether to take it literally.

'He is real,' his dad said. 'The Bible is clear about that. But there are two mistakes people make about him.'

'What are they?' Marco asked.

'The first is to ignore him completely, as if he does not exist or does not matter. The second is to be obsessed with him, giving him more attention and power than he deserves.'

'So what is the right way to think about him?' Marco asked.

'Take him seriously without fearing him,' his dad said. 'He is real, he is dangerous, and he hates everything God loves. But he is not equal to God. He is a defeated enemy who has not yet accepted his defeat. And for anyone in Christ, the outcome is already decided.'

Who Is Satan?

Satan is a real spiritual being. He is not a cartoon character or a symbol of evil. He is a personal being who actively opposes God and works against His people.

The name Satan means adversary or accuser. He is also called the devil, which means slanderer. First Peter 5:8 says he prowls around like a roaring lion looking for someone to devour.

But Satan is not the opposite of God. God has no equal. Satan is a created being who turned against his Creator.

Where Did Satan Come From?

Satan was originally a powerful angel who rebelled against God. Isaiah 14:12-15 and Ezekiel 28:12-17 are often read as describing his fall, though scholars note these passages also address human rulers directly.

What is clear throughout Scripture is that Satan chose pride and rebellion over submission to God. He was removed from his exalted position. He did not fall accidentally. He chose to rebel.

Jesus said in Luke 10:18 that He saw Satan fall like lightning from heaven.

What Satan Can and Cannot Do

Satan is powerful, but he has real limits.

He cannot read your mind. He is not all-knowing. He cannot be everywhere at once. He is not all-present.

Most importantly, he is already defeated. Colossians 2:15 says Jesus disarmed the powers and authorities and triumphed over them at the cross.

Satan still acts. He still tempts and accuses. But he acts as a defeated enemy. His end is already settled. (Revelation 20:10.) For those in Christ, he has no ultimate claim.

Key Verses

"Be alert and of sober mind. Your enemy the devil prowls around like a roaring lion looking for someone to devour." (1 Peter 5:8)

"Having disarmed the powers and authorities, he made a public spectacle of them, triumphing over them by the cross." (Colossians 2:15)

This Week's Verse to Memorize

Colossians 2:15

"Having disarmed the powers and authorities, he made a public spectacle of them, triumphing over them by the cross."

This verse says the defeat of Satan happened at the cross. It is past tense. Done. Write it out and underline the word 'triumphing.' What does it mean for your daily life that Jesus has already won?

Activities

Activity 1: Two Mistakes

Marco's dad described two wrong ways to think about Satan: ignoring him completely or being obsessed with him. In your journal, write one paragraph about the dangers of each mistake. Then write one sentence describing the healthy middle position.

Activity 2: What He Can and Cannot Do

Based on what you learned this week, make a two-column chart. Label one column What Satan Can Do and the other What Satan Cannot Do. Fill in each column from Scripture and from what you learned. Then write one sentence about how this knowledge changes the way you think about temptation.

Quiz Time

Answer these questions in your journal or workbook:

1. What does the name Satan mean?

2. Is Satan equal to God? Explain.

3. What does 1 Peter 5:8 compare Satan to?

4. According to Colossians 2:15, what happened to Satan at the cross?

5. What are two things Satan cannot do?

This Week's Challenge

This week, when you feel tempted or discouraged, say out loud: Jesus has already won. Satan is defeated. I belong to Christ. This is not a magic formula. It is a reminder of what is true. Write about what happened when you said it.

New Words to Know

Satan: A real spiritual being who opposes God and His people. The name means adversary or accuser.

Devil: Another name for Satan. It means slanderer, one who lies and accuses falsely.

Fallen Angel: An angel who rebelled against God. Satan is the most prominent example. Demons are generally understood to be fallen angels.

Defeated Enemy: A description of Satan's true status. He still acts, but Christ's victory at the cross has already determined his end.

Week 37: What Is Spiritual Warfare?

How do I actually fight a battle I cannot see?

Zoe had been feeling pulled in two directions all week.

She knew what she believed. She knew what was right. But the temptation to go along with what her friends were doing kept coming back.

She told her youth leader about it.

'That is spiritual warfare,' her leader said.

'I thought spiritual warfare was something dramatic,' Zoe said. 'Like in movies.'

'Sometimes it is dramatic,' her leader said. 'But most of the time it looks exactly like what you just described. A quiet pressure to drift from what you know is true. A temptation that keeps returning. A whisper that says it does not really matter.'

'So what do I do?' Zoe asked.

'The Bible gives you specific tools,' her leader said. 'And the most important thing to remember is that you are not fighting for victory. You are fighting from victory. Jesus already won. You are just holding the ground He secured.'

We Are in a Real Battle

The Bible is honest that Christians are in a spiritual battle. Ephesians 6:12 says we do not wrestle against flesh and blood, but against spiritual forces of evil in the heavenly realms.

This means the real enemy is not the person who annoys you or hurts you. Spiritual forces work to pull people away from God, from truth, and from each other.

Knowing this changes how we respond to temptation and hardship.

The Armor of God

Ephesians 6:13-17 gives believers a specific set of spiritual resources, described as armor. Each piece represents something real.

The belt of truth: knowing what is true keeps everything else in place.

The breastplate of righteousness: living rightly protects your heart from accusation.

Feet fitted with the gospel of peace: being grounded in the gospel gives you stability.

The shield of faith: trusting God deflects attacks of doubt and fear.

The helmet of salvation: knowing you are saved protects your mind.

The sword of the Spirit: the Word of God, the only offensive weapon in the list.

Fighting from Victory

The most important thing to understand about spiritual warfare is that Jesus has already won.

Colossians 2:15 says Jesus disarmed the powers at the cross and triumphed over them. The battle is real, but the outcome is settled.

First John 4:4 says the one who is in you is greater than the one who is in the world. The Holy Spirit, who lives in every believer, is more powerful than any spiritual force working against them.

We resist. We stand firm. We use the tools God provides. But we do it from a position of victory, not desperation.

Key Verses

"For our struggle is not against flesh and blood, but against the rulers, against the authorities, against the powers of this dark world and against the spiritual forces of evil in the heavenly realms." (Ephesians 6:12)

"You, dear children, are from God and have overcome them, because the one who is in you is greater than the one who is in the world." (1 John 4:4)

This Week's Verse to Memorize

1 John 4:4

"You, dear children, are from God and have overcome them, because the one who is in you is greater than the one who is in the world."

The greater one living in you is the Holy Spirit. Write this verse out and say it slowly. Then write one situation in your life right now where you need to remember that the one in you is greater.

Activities

Activity 1: Armor Inventory

Read Ephesians 6:10-18. For each piece of armor, write what it represents and one practical way you could put it on this week. For example, putting on the belt of truth might mean memorizing a Bible verse about something you have been doubting.

Activity 2: Identifying the Real Battle

Think of a conflict or struggle you faced this week. In your journal, write about it from two angles: the surface level (what it looked like on the outside) and the spiritual level (what might have been happening underneath). How does Ephesians 6:12 change how you see that situation?

Quiz Time

Answer these questions in your journal or workbook:

1. According to Ephesians 6:12, who is our real enemy?

2. Name three pieces of the armor of God and what each one represents.

3. What is the only offensive weapon in the armor of God?

4. According to 1 John 4:4, who is greater: the Spirit in you or the enemy in the world?

5. What does it mean to fight from victory rather than for victory?

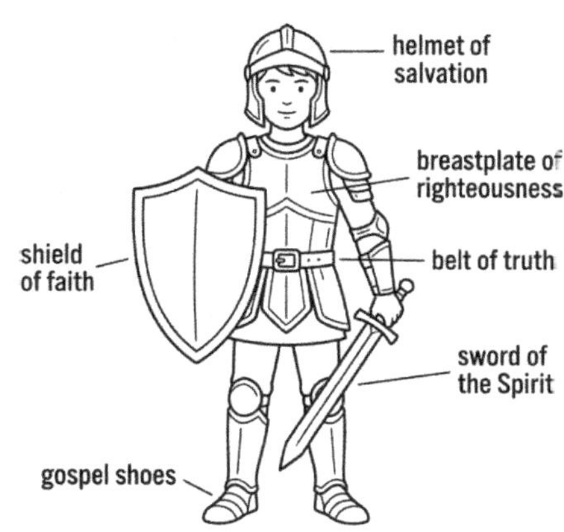

Standing Firm in Christ

This Week's Challenge

Read Ephesians 6:10-18 every morning this week. Each day, pick one piece of armor and think about how you will put it on specifically that day. By the end of the week you will have gone through all six. Write one sentence each day about what you noticed.

New Words to Know

Spiritual Warfare: The real but unseen battle between God's kingdom and the forces of evil. Christians participate in it through prayer, truth, faith, and the Word of God.

Armor of God: The spiritual resources Paul describes in Ephesians 6 that believers use to stand firm against spiritual opposition.

Resist: To actively stand against something. James 4:7 says to resist the devil and he will flee. Resistance is active, not passive.

Victory in Christ: The truth that Jesus's death and resurrection have already decided the outcome of the spiritual battle. Believers fight from this settled victory.

Eleven

The End Times

Weeks 38 through 41

Death, heaven, hell, and the return of Christ. What does the Bible actually teach? Four weeks on the last things, grounded in hope.

Weeks in this chapter:

- Week 38: What Happens When We Die?
- Week 39: What Is Heaven?
- Week 40: What Is Hell?
- Week 41: What Is the Second Coming?

Week 38: What Happens When We Die?

Is death the end, or is there something more?

Grandma passed away on a Tuesday morning.

Lily had known it was coming. But that did not make it easier.

At the funeral, her uncle said something she kept thinking about afterward.

'She is not gone,' he said. 'She is more alive right now than she ever was here.'

Lily asked her mom about it on the drive home.

'What did he mean? Where is she?'

Her mom was quiet for a moment. 'The Bible teaches that when a believer dies, they go to be with Jesus right away. Their body is buried, but they are not in the body anymore. They are with Him. And one day, their body will be raised and made new, and they will be with Him completely and forever.'

'So death is not the end?' Lily asked.

'For someone who trusts Jesus,' her mom said, 'death is a door, not a wall.'

Physical Death Is Not the End

Death entered the world through sin. (Romans 5:12.) It was not part of God's original design.

But for believers, death has lost its final power. First Corinthians 15:55 says: Where, O death, is your victory? Where, O death, is your sting?

Jesus conquered death by rising from the dead. Because He lives, those who belong to Him will also live.

What Happens Immediately After Death?

The Bible teaches that at death, the soul separates from the body. For believers, this means going immediately to be with Christ.

Philippians 1:23 says Paul desired to depart and be with Christ, which is better by far. Second Corinthians 5:8 says to be absent from the body is to be present with the Lord.

For the believer, death is a door, not a wall.

This state between death and the final resurrection is called the intermediate state. Believers are with Jesus, conscious and at peace, but it is not yet the final destination.

The Resurrection of the Body

One day, Jesus will return and the dead will be raised. This is not just the soul going to heaven. It is the body being raised and transformed.

First Corinthians 15:42-44 describes resurrection bodies as imperishable, glorious, and powerful. Not ghostly, but real and new.

This is the final hope. Not escaping the body, but having the body made completely new. God redeems all of us, body and soul.

Key Verses

"For to me, to live is Christ and to die is gain." (Philippians 1:21)

"Where, O death, is your victory? Where, O death, is your sting?" (1 Corinthians 15:55)

This Week's Verse to Memorize

Philippians 1:21

"For to me, to live is Christ and to die is gain."

Paul wrote this from prison. He was not afraid of death because he knew what was waiting. Write this verse out and then write one sentence about what it means for death to be 'gain' for a believer.

Activities

Activity 1: Three Stages

In your journal, draw a simple timeline with three points. Label them: Now (life in the body), Intermediate State (after death, before resurrection), and Final Resurrection (body raised and made new). For each point, write one or two sentences describing what the Bible says about that stage, using the verses from this week.

Activity 2: Letters from Paul

Read Philippians 1:20-24. Paul is wrestling with whether he wants to live or die. Write a short paragraph explaining why Paul is not afraid to die, based on what he says in those verses. Then write one sentence about what his attitude tells you about what he believed happens after death.

Quiz Time

Answer these questions in your journal or workbook:

1. Where did death come from, according to Romans 5:12?

2. According to Philippians 1:23 and 2 Corinthians 5:8, where do believers go immediately after death?

3. What is the intermediate state?

4. What will happen to bodies at the resurrection?

5. How does 1 Corinthians 15:55 describe death's power over believers?

This Week's Challenge

If you have lost someone you love, write them a letter this week in your journal. Tell them what you miss and what you are looking forward to if you will see them again. If you have not lost anyone close yet, write about what comforts you most about what you learned this week.

New Words to Know

Intermediate State: The condition of the soul between physical death and the final resurrection. Believers are with Christ; the body awaits resurrection.

Resurrection: The raising of the physical body from death, transformed and made imperishable. This is the final hope for every believer.

Soul: The non-physical part of a person that continues to exist after the body dies.

Immortality: Living forever. Only God is inherently immortal. Believers receive immortality as a gift through Jesus Christ.

Week 39: What Is Heaven?

Is heaven just sitting on clouds forever? What does the Bible actually say?

'What is heaven actually like?' Theo asked his dad.

'Is it just sitting on clouds playing harps forever?'

His dad smiled. 'Not even close. That image does not come from the Bible. It comes from cartoons.'

'Then what does the Bible say?'

'It says God will make everything new. Not destroy everything and replace it with something totally different. Renew it. Fix it. Restore it to what it was always meant to be. The last two chapters of the Bible describe a city, a garden, a place of real life with real people in a real world, but one where everything wrong has been made right.'

'So it is like Earth, but better?' Theo asked.

'Much better,' his dad said. 'And the best part is not the place. It is the person. Being fully with God, with no sin in the way. That is what makes it heaven.'

Heaven Is a Real Place

Heaven is not a vague spiritual state. It is a real destination. Jesus said in John 14:2-3 that He is going to prepare a place for His followers and will come back to take them there.

The word place is significant. Jesus does not say He is preparing a feeling or an experience. He is preparing somewhere.

The New Creation

The Bible's fullest description of our final home is not heaven floating in the clouds. It is the new creation.

Revelation 21:1-5 describes a new heaven and a new earth. God will make all things new. The New Jerusalem comes down from God to earth. Heaven comes to earth.

This new creation is physical, beautiful, and permanent. It is not an escape from the world. It is the world redeemed and restored.

What Makes Heaven Heaven

The most important feature of heaven is not its beauty or its lack of pain. It is the presence of God.

Revelation 21:3 says God's dwelling place will be with people. He will live with them. That is the core promise.

First Corinthians 13:12 says we will know fully, even as we are fully known. The partial knowledge of God we have now will give way to clear, direct knowing.

Every good thing we love in this world, beauty, friendship, creativity, joy, will be there in its fullest form. All good things come from God, and in heaven we will be fully with Him.

Key Verses

"My Father's house has many rooms; if that were not so, would I have told you that I am going there to prepare a place for you?" (John 14:2)

"He will wipe every tear from their eyes. There will be no more death or mourning or crying or pain." (Revelation 21:4)

This Week's Verse to Memorize

Revelation 21:4

"He will wipe every tear from their eyes. There will be no more death or mourning or crying or pain, for the old order of things has passed away."

This verse lists four things that will be gone. Write them down. Then write about which one means the most to you personally and why.

Activities

Activity 1: Read Revelation 21-22

Read Revelation 21:1 through 22:5. This is the Bible's most detailed picture of our final home. List seven specific things John describes about the new creation. Then write one sentence about what surprised you most.

Activity 2: What I Am Looking Forward To

Based on what you learned this week, write a paragraph about three things you are genuinely looking forward to about heaven. Be specific. Not just no more pain, but what that will actually mean. Let yourself feel the hope.

Quiz Time

Answer these questions in your journal or workbook:

Not clouds and harps. A real world, fully redeemed.

1. According to John 14:2-3, what is Jesus doing right now?

2. What does Revelation 21 describe as our final destination?

3. Is the new creation physical or purely spiritual?

4. According to Revelation 21:3, what is the central promise about heaven?

5. Name three things Revelation 21:4 says will no longer exist in the new creation.

This Week's Challenge

This week, when you enjoy something beautiful, something that makes you genuinely happy, pause and say: this is a preview. This is God showing me a shadow of what is coming. Write down three moments from this week that felt like previews of heaven and explain why.

New Words to Know

New Creation: The final state of all things after God renews the heavens and the earth. Physical, beautiful, and permanent.

New Jerusalem: The city described in Revelation 21-22 that comes down from heaven to earth. It represents the fullness of God's dwelling with His people.

Eternal Life: Not just life that goes on forever, but a new quality of life in full relationship with God. It begins now and continues into the new creation.

Beatific Vision: A theological term for the direct experience of seeing and knowing God face to face that believers will have in heaven.

Week 40: What Is Hell?

Why would a loving God allow anyone to go to hell?

'Do people really go to hell?' Marcus asked his youth leader.

'It is one of the hardest things in the Bible to think about,' his leader said. 'But yes. Jesus talked about it more than anyone else in Scripture.'

'Why would a loving God send people there?'

His leader thought for a moment. 'Think about it this way. God does not force anyone to love Him or be with Him. He gives people the choice. Hell is, at its core, the permanent consequence of choosing to live apart from God. It is not something God wants. Second Peter 3:9 says He does not want anyone to perish.'

'Then why does it exist?'

'Because love requires a real choice. God will not override someone's rejection of Him forever. If someone spends their whole life saying: I do not want God, at the end, He honors that choice. And a life without God, permanently, is what hell is.'

Marcus was quiet. 'That makes it sound even more serious.'

'It is,' his leader said. 'That is exactly why the gospel matters so much.'

Hell Is Real

Hell is one of the most difficult topics in Christian theology. But it is also one that Jesus addressed directly and seriously.

Matthew 25:46 says the wicked will go away to eternal punishment. Revelation 20:15 describes the lake of fire. Jesus used these images to warn people urgently, not casually.

The Bible's clearest description of hell is not a torture chamber. It is separation from God. Second Thessalonians 1:9

says those who reject God will be shut out from the presence of the Lord.

Why Does Hell Exist?

God does not want anyone to go to hell. Second Peter 3:9 says He is patient, not wanting anyone to perish, but everyone to come to repentance.

Hell exists because God takes human choice seriously. He will not force anyone into a relationship with Him. For those who spend their lives rejecting God, hell is the permanent result of that rejection.

This is not a popular teaching. But it is what Jesus taught, and it is one of the strongest reasons the gospel matters.

The Urgency of the Gospel

Understanding hell honestly makes the gospel more precious, not less.

If there were no consequences for rejecting God, the rescue Jesus provides would not feel urgent. But because the stakes are real, the good news is genuinely good news.

THE MOST SERIOUS CHOICE ANYONE WILL EVER MAKE

John 3:16 says God gave His one and only Son so that whoever believes in Him shall not perish but have eternal life. The offer is real. The need is real. And the answer is Jesus.

Key Verses

"The Lord is not slow in keeping his promise, as some understand slowness. Instead, he is patient with you, not wanting anyone to perish, but everyone to come to repentance." (2 Peter 3:9)

"For God so loved the world that he gave his one and only Son, that whoever believes in him shall not perish but have eternal life." (John 3:16)

This Week's Verse to Memorize

2 Peter 3:9

"The Lord is not slow in keeping his promise, as some understand slowness. Instead he is patient with you, not wanting anyone to perish, but everyone to come to repentance."

This verse tells us what God wants. He wants everyone to repent. Write it out, and then write one sentence about what it says about God's heart toward people who have not yet trusted Him.

Activities

Activity 1: What Jesus Said

Read Matthew 25:31-46. Jesus tells a story about a final judgment. Write down three things this passage teaches about how people will be judged. Then write one sentence about how this passage makes you feel and what you want to do in response.

Activity 2: The Right Response

Some people respond to the doctrine of hell with fear. Others respond with increased urgency to share the gospel. Write a paragraph about what you think the right response is, using at least two Bible verses from this week to support your answer.

Quiz Time

Answer these questions in your journal or workbook:

1. Who talked about hell more than anyone else in the Bible?

2. What is the Bible's clearest description of hell?

3. According to 2 Peter 3:9, does God want people to go to hell?

4. Why does hell exist, according to what you learned this week?

5. How does understanding hell make the gospel more important?

This Week's Challenge

Think of one person in your life who does not know Jesus. Write their name in your journal and commit to praying for them every day this week. You do not need to say anything to them yet. Just pray. Let the weight of this week's teaching turn into love for that person.

New Words to Know

Hell: The permanent state of separation from God that results from rejecting Him. The Bible's primary description is exclusion from God's presence.

Judgment: God's final reckoning with every person's choices and actions. It is both just and consistent with His character.

Eternal Punishment: The description Jesus uses in Matthew 25:46 for the final state of those who reject God. It is permanent.

Repentance: Turning to God. Second Peter 3:9 says God is patient because He wants everyone to have the opportunity to repent.

Week 41: What Is the Second Coming?

Is Jesus really coming back? And how should that change how I live?

'Is Jesus really coming back?' Sophie asked her pastor.

'He is,' he said. 'That is one of the most certain promises in all of Scripture.'

'When?'

'Nobody knows. Jesus said in Matthew 24:36 that not even the angels knew the day or the hour. Only the Father knows.'

'Does that bother you?' Sophie asked.

'Not anymore,' her pastor said. 'I used to want to know the timeline. But the more I read Scripture, the more I see that the point is not when. The point is that He is coming and we should be ready. That is the focus Jesus keeps returning to. Not: figure out the date. But: live ready.'

Sophie thought about that. 'What does living ready look like?'

'Loving God. Loving people. Sharing the gospel. Serving faithfully. Doing what He said to do while we wait for Him to return.'

Jesus Is Coming Back

The return of Jesus is one of the most repeated promises in the New Testament. Acts 1:11 says Jesus will come back in the same way He was seen going into heaven.

His return will be visible, physical, and unmistakable. It will not be quiet or hidden.

What Will Happen When He Returns?

Several things will happen at Christ's return.

The dead in Christ will be raised first, their bodies transformed and reunited with their souls. (1 Thessalonians 4:16.)

Those alive when He returns will also be transformed. (1 Corinthians 15:51-52.)

There will be a final judgment. Every person will stand before God, and the books will be opened. (Revelation 20:12-13.)

The new creation will be fully established. God makes everything new and dwells with His people forever.

Living in Light of His Return

The Bible does not give a detailed timeline of exactly what will happen and when. Christians disagree on many of those details, and this workbook does not take sides in those debates.

What Scripture is clear about is how we should live while we wait.

Matthew 24:44 says to be ready, because the Son of Man will come at an hour when you do not expect Him.

Second Peter 3:11-12 asks what kind of people we ought to be in light of His coming. The answer is: holy and godly, looking forward to that day.

We wait with hope. We live with purpose. We hold the future loosely, trusting the One who holds it.

Key Verses

"This same Jesus, who has been taken from you into heaven, will come back in the same way you have seen him go into heaven." (Acts 1:11)

"Therefore keep watch, because you do not know on what day your Lord will come." (Matthew 24:42)

This Week's Verse to Memorize

Acts 1:11

"This same Jesus, who has been taken from you into heaven, will come back in the same way you have seen him go into heaven."

The same Jesus who walked the earth and rose from the dead is the one who is coming back. Write this verse out and circle the words 'same Jesus.' What does it mean to you that it is Him specifically who is returning?

Activities

Activity 1: What We Know for Certain

Make a two-column chart. Label one column What the Bible Clearly Says About the Second Coming and the other column What the Bible Does Not Tell Us. Fill in both columns from what you learned this week. What belongs in each column tells you where to focus your attention.

Activity 2: Living Ready

Read Matthew 25:14-30, the parable of the talents. Jesus tells this story to describe what it means to be ready for His return. Write three practical ways you could live more faithfully right now in light of Jesus coming back. Be specific and personal, not general.

Quiz Time

Answer these questions in your journal or workbook:

1. According to Acts 1:11, how will Jesus return?

2. According to Matthew 24:36, who knows the day and hour of Christ's return?

3. Name two things that will happen when Jesus returns.

4. What does Matthew 24:44 tell us to do while we wait?

5. What does 2 Peter 3:11-12 say we should be like in light of Christ's return?

This Week's Challenge

Write a one-paragraph answer to this question in your journal: If Jesus came back today, what would you be glad you spent your time on this week? And what would you wish you had done differently? Let your answers shape how you spend next week.

New Words to Know

Second Coming: The return of Jesus Christ to earth, bodily and visibly, to judge the living and the dead and establish the new creation fully.

Final Judgment: God's ultimate reckoning with every person's choices. It is described in Revelation 20 and Matthew 25.

Eschatology: The branch of theology that studies the end times and last things. From the Greek word eschatos, meaning last.

Imminence: The teaching that Jesus could return at any time. Because no one knows the day or hour, every generation should live as if His return could happen soon.

Twelve

Living a Christian Life

Weeks 42 through 52

Everything learned, now lived. Eleven weeks on following Jesus in the ordinary moments of an ordinary life.

Weeks in this unit:

- Week 42: What Does It Mean to Follow Jesus Daily?
- Week 43: Reading and Understanding the Bible
- Week 44: Loving God and Loving Others
- Week 45: Forgiveness: Giving and Receiving
- Week 46: Serving Others
- Week 47: Sharing Your Faith
- Week 48: Dealing with Doubt
- Week 49: Suffering and Faith
- Week 50: Money, Generosity, and Stewardship
- Week 51: Rest, Sabbath, and Margin
- Week 52: A Life of Faith: Putting It All Together

Week 42: What Does It Mean to Follow Jesus Daily?

Is following Jesus a one-time decision or something you do every day?

Marcus had given his life to Jesus six months ago.

But lately he had a nagging feeling that nothing had really changed.

He told his youth leader about it.

'I thought being a Christian would feel different,' he said. 'More dramatic. But most days feel exactly the same as before.'

His leader nodded. 'Following Jesus is not a feeling. It is a direction. It is not one big moment but a thousand small choices pointing the same way.'

'What kind of choices?' Marcus asked.

'Every morning you wake up and decide: am I going to live for myself today, or for God? That decision shows up in how you treat people, what you say, what you look at, how you spend your time. None of those moments feel dramatic. But together, over a lifetime, they become a life.'

Following Jesus Is a Daily Choice

Jesus said in Luke 9:23: If anyone wants to follow me, let him deny himself and take up his cross daily and follow me.

The word daily is important. Following Jesus is not a one-time decision that runs on autopilot. It is a direction chosen again every morning.

This does not mean you earn your salvation every day. It means that salvation produces a life of ongoing, active following.

What Daily Discipleship Looks Like

Discipleship is the word the Bible uses for following Jesus. A disciple is a learner and a follower.

It looks like spending time with God through prayer and Scripture. It looks like making choices that reflect your values. It looks like staying connected to other believers. It looks like serving and giving and forgiving.

None of these things are dramatic in the moment. But they compound over time. A year of small daily faithfulness produces a person who looks noticeably more like Jesus.

Growing Is Not the Same as Being Perfect

One of the most important things to understand is that growth is not perfection.

You will fail. You will sin. You will have days when you feel spiritually dry. That is normal. First John 1:9 says that when we confess our sins, He forgives and cleanses us.

What matters is not that you never fall. It is that you keep getting up and keep moving in the right direction.

Key Verses

"If anyone wants to follow me, let him deny himself and take up his cross daily and follow me." (Luke 9:23)

"Being confident of this, that he who began a good work in you will carry it on to completion until the day of Christ Jesus." (Philippians 1:6)

This Week's Verse to Memorize

Luke 9:23

"If anyone wants to follow me, let him deny himself and take up his cross daily and follow me."

Notice the word 'daily.' Write this verse out and then write one sentence about what it means in your own life to take up your cross today, not just once.

Activities

A THOUSAND SMALL CHOICES. ONE DIRECTION. A LIFE OF FAITH.

Activity 1: Your Spiritual Autobiography

Write a short personal history of your faith so far. When did you first hear about Jesus? What has your journey looked like since then? What is one specific way you have grown? This is not a report. It is your story. Be honest and personal.

Activity 2: What Does Today Look Like?

Think about a typical Tuesday in your life. Write down your schedule from morning to night. Then next to each activity, write one sentence about how following Jesus could shape the way you approach it. What would change? What would stay the same?

Quiz Time

Answer these questions in your journal or workbook:

1. What does the word 'daily' in Luke 9:23 tell us about following Jesus?

2. What is a disciple?

3. Name three things daily discipleship looks like in practice.

4. According to 1 John 1:9, what happens when we confess our sins?

5. What is the difference between growth and perfection in the Christian life?

This Week's Challenge

This week, start each morning with one simple sentence before you get out of bed: 'Today I choose to follow You.' Say it even when you do not feel like it. Write at the end of the week about whether it made a difference.

New Words to Know

Disciple: A follower and learner of Jesus. All Christians are disciples.

Discipleship: The ongoing process of following Jesus, learning from Him, and becoming more like Him.

Daily Cross: Jesus's phrase in Luke 9:23 for the daily choice to deny yourself and follow Him.

Sanctification: The Holy Spirit's work of making you more like Jesus over time. It is a process, not an instant change.

Week 43: Reading and Understanding the Bible

How do I actually read the Bible in a way that changes me?

Sophie had been trying to read her Bible every day.

But she kept getting stuck. She would open it, read a few verses, feel nothing, and close it again.

'Am I doing it wrong?' she asked her pastor.

'You are doing it,' he said. 'That is already more than most people. But let me ask: what are you looking for when you open it?'

Sophie thought about it. 'I do not know. Information, maybe?'

'Try looking for God instead,' her pastor said. 'The Bible is not primarily a rulebook or a history book. It is a letter from someone who loves you. When you read it, ask: what does this tell me about who God is? What does He want me to know? What does He want me to do? Those three questions will change everything about how you read.'

The Bible Is a Letter, Not Just a Book

We covered where the Bible came from in Unit 3. Now we focus on how to actually read it well.

Second Timothy 3:16-17 says Scripture is useful for teaching, rebuking, correcting, and training in righteousness. It has practical purpose. It is meant to shape you, not just inform you.

The key is to read expecting to meet God, not just gather information.

Three Questions to Ask Every Time You Read

These three questions work for any passage in any book of the Bible.

What does this tell me about God? Every passage reveals something about who He is, what He values, or how He acts.

What does this tell me about people? The Bible is honest about human nature, both its greatness and its brokenness.

What does this tell me about how to live? Some passages are direct commands. Others are examples. Others are promises. All of them have something to teach about life.

Not just reading. Meeting God.

Practical Habits for Reading Well

Start small. Five minutes of focused reading beats thirty minutes of distracted skimming.

Read whole books, not just random verses. A verse taken out of context can mean almost anything. A verse in context means what the author intended.

Write down one thing you noticed. Psalm 119:11 says God's word hidden in the heart guards against sin. Writing helps you hide it there.

Pray before you read. Ask the Holy Spirit, who inspired the Word, to help you understand it. He is the best Bible teacher available.

Key Verses

"All Scripture is God-breathed and is useful for teaching, rebuking, correcting and training in righteousness." (2 Timothy 3:16)

"I have hidden your word in my heart that I might not sin against you." (Psalm 119:11)

This Week's Verse to Memorize

Psalm 119:11

"I have hidden your word in my heart that I might not sin against you."

Hiding the word in your heart means more than memorizing it. It means letting it shape you from the inside. Write this verse and then write one verse you have memorized and what it means to you.

Activities

Activity 1: Three-Question Journal

Choose any passage of the Bible, at least ten verses. Read it slowly. Then answer all three questions in your journal: What does this tell me about God? What does this tell me about people? What does this tell me about how to live? Do this with the same passage three days in a row and notice what new things you see each time.

Activity 2: Your Bible Reading Plan

Design a simple Bible reading plan for the next thirty days. Choose one book of the Bible to read through. Figure out how many chapters you would need to read each day to finish it. Write the plan out and then start it this week. Consistency matters more than speed.

Quiz Time

Answer these questions in your journal or workbook:

1. According to 2 Timothy 3:16-17, what is Scripture useful for?

2. What is the difference between reading for information and reading to meet God?

3. What are the three questions to ask every time you read the Bible?

4. Why is it better to read whole books than random verses?

5. According to Psalm 119:11, what does hiding God's word in your heart do?

This Week's Challenge

Read the same short passage every day this week, something like Psalm 23 or John 15:1-11. Each day, write down one new thing you notice. By the end of the week you will have seven observations from the same text. See how your understanding deepens with repeated reading.

New Words to Know

Exegesis: The practice of drawing out the meaning of a text by studying it carefully in its context.

Context: The surrounding verses, chapter, and book that help you understand what a specific passage means.

Devotional Reading: Reading the Bible with the goal of hearing from God personally, not just understanding it academically.

Meditation: Thinking deeply about a passage over time, turning it over in your mind, letting it settle into your heart.

Week 44: Loving God and Loving Others

If the whole Christian life can be summed up in two commands, what are they and how do I live them?

A teacher once asked Jesus which commandment was the greatest.

Jesus did not hesitate. Love God with everything you have. And love your neighbor as yourself. Everything else, He said, hangs on these two.

Priya's Sunday school class had been discussing what that meant in practice.

'It sounds simple,' said one student.

'It is simple,' Priya said. 'It is just not easy.'

Her teacher smiled. 'That is exactly right. The Great Commandment is not complicated. But living it out costs you something every single day.'

'What does it cost?' another student asked.

'Your comfort. Your time. Your pride. Your preferences. Loving God means putting Him first when you would rather put yourself first. Loving people means treating them the way you want to be treated, even when they do not deserve it. That is where the cost comes in.'

The Greatest Commandment

In Matthew 22:37-40, Jesus sums up the entire law in two commands. Love the Lord your God with all your heart, soul, and mind. And love your neighbor as yourself.

These two commands flow from each other. You cannot genuinely love God and hate people. Love for people flows from a heart that has been changed by knowing God.

First John 4:20 says: If anyone says I love God, yet hates his brother, he is a liar. Love for God shows up in love for people.

Loving God with Everything

Loving God with all your heart, soul, and mind means He gets the best of you, not the leftovers.

It means your first thought in the morning is not your schedule but Him. It means your biggest concern is not disappointing people but grieving Him. It means your deepest desire is knowing Him, not just knowing about Him.

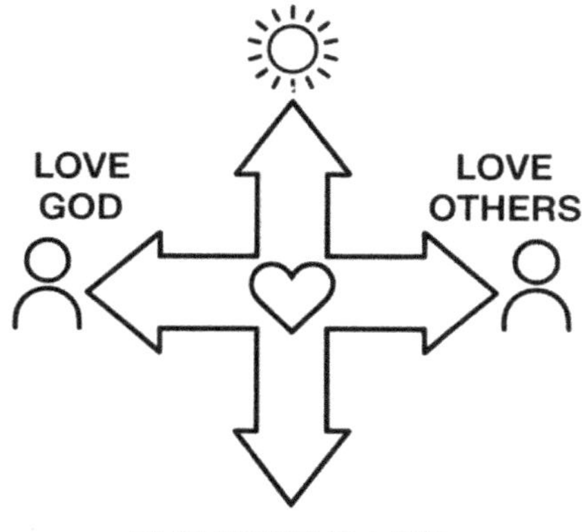

This is a lifelong pursuit, not an achievement. None of us arrives. But the direction of our hearts matters.

Loving Your Neighbor

Jesus was once asked: who is my neighbor? He answered with the parable of the Good Samaritan in Luke 10:30-37. The neighbor was not the person who shared the same background or beliefs. It was the person who showed up and helped.

Your neighbor is whoever is in front of you and in need. Loving them means acting, not just feeling warmly toward them.

Romans 13:10 says love is the fulfillment of the law. Everything God asks of us can be traced back to love.

Key Verses

"Love the Lord your God with all your heart and with all your soul and with all your mind. This is the first and greatest commandment. And the second is like it: love your neighbor as yourself." (Matthew 22:37-39)

"Whoever claims to love God yet hates a brother or sister is a liar." (1 John 4:20)

This Week's Verse to Memorize

Matthew 22:37

"Love the Lord your God with all your heart and with all your soul and with all your mind."

This is the greatest commandment. Write it out and then write one honest sentence about which part of you is hardest to give fully to God: your heart, your soul, or your mind.

Activities

Activity 1: Neighbor Map

Draw a simple map of your world: home, school, neighborhood, church, activities. Mark the people in each area. Then circle three people you have not loved well recently. Write one specific thing you could do for each of them this week to love them more like Jesus does.

Activity 2: Heart Check

Matthew 22:37 says to love God with heart, soul, and mind. In your journal, give yourself an honest score from one to ten for each area. Heart: how much do you desire God emotionally? Soul: how much does your inner life belong to Him? Mind: how much do your thoughts revolve around Him? Then write one practical step to grow in your lowest area.

Quiz Time

Answer these questions in your journal or workbook:

1. What are the two greatest commandments according to Jesus in Matthew 22?

2. How are the two commandments connected to each other?

3. What does 1 John 4:20 say about someone who claims to love God but hates others?

4. Who is your neighbor, according to the parable of the Good Samaritan?

5. According to Romans 13:10, what is love the fulfillment of?

This Week's Challenge

Choose one person this week who is difficult for you to love. Pray for them every day. Do one kind thing for them by the end of the week. It does not need to be big. Write about how it felt before and after.

New Words to Know

Great Commandment: Jesus's summary of the entire law in Matthew 22:37-40. Love God with everything. Love your neighbor as yourself.

Neighbor: In Jesus's teaching, your neighbor is anyone who is near you and in need, regardless of background.

Agape: The Greek word for the self-giving love that God shows and commands. It is a choice, not just a feeling.

Fulfillment of the Law: Paul's phrase in Romans 13:10. Love does not replace the law. It is what the law was always pointing toward.

Week 45: Forgiveness: Giving and Receiving

Do I have to forgive someone who has never said sorry?

Eli had not spoken to his best friend in three weeks.

His friend had said something that hurt, and Eli had decided to wait for an apology before moving on.

The apology had not come.

His dad noticed the tension. 'Have you forgiven him?' he asked.

'He has not apologized,' Eli said.

'That is not what I asked,' his dad said. 'Forgiveness and reconciliation are two different things. Reconciliation requires both people. Forgiveness is something you do in your own heart, whether or not the other person ever says sorry.'

'Then what is the point of forgiving if nothing changes between us?' Eli asked.

'It changes you,' his dad said. 'Holding onto unforgiveness is like drinking poison and waiting for the other person to get sick. Forgiveness releases you. It does not excuse what they did. It just means you are not going to let it own you anymore.'

What Forgiveness Is and Is Not

Forgiveness is not saying what happened did not matter. It is not pretending you were not hurt. It is not automatic trust or instant reconciliation.

Forgiveness is a choice to release the debt. To say: I am not going to hold this against you anymore. I am going to let God handle the justice.

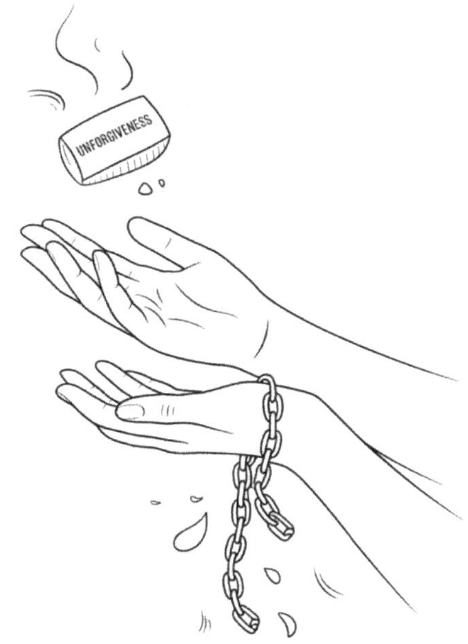

Colossians 3:13 says: Bear with each other and forgive one another if any of you has a grievance against someone. Forgive as the Lord forgave you.

Why We Forgive

The reason Christians forgive is not because it feels good or because it is fair. It is because we have been forgiven an unpayable debt.

Jesus told a parable in Matthew 18:21-35 about a servant forgiven an enormous debt who then refused to forgive a small one. Those who have received great forgiveness have no excuse for withholding small forgiveness.

Ephesians 4:32 says: Be kind and compassionate to one another, forgiving each other, just as in Christ God forgave you.

Receiving Forgiveness

Many people find it easier to forgive others than to receive forgiveness themselves.

First John 1:9 promises that if we confess our sins, God is faithful and just to forgive us and cleanse us from all unrighteousness. This is not a vague hope. It is a promise.

Carrying guilt that God has already removed is not humility. It is unbelief. Receiving His forgiveness means trusting that what He says is true: it is finished, and you are clean.

Key Verses

"Bear with each other and forgive one another if any of you has a grievance against someone. Forgive as the Lord forgave you." (Colossians 3:13)

"Be kind and compassionate to one another, forgiving each other, just as in Christ God forgave you." (Ephesians 4:32)

This Week's Verse to Memorize

Colossians 3:13

"Forgive as the Lord forgave you."

This is the standard. Not forgiving when you feel like it. Forgiving the way God forgave you. Write this verse out and then write one sentence about what it means that God's forgiveness of you is the model for your forgiveness of others.

Activities

Activity 1: Forgiveness vs Reconciliation

In your journal, explain the difference between forgiveness and reconciliation in your own words. Then think of a situation where you forgave someone but reconciliation was not possible or safe. What did forgiveness look like in that situation? What did it not include?

Activity 2: A Letter You May Never Send

Think of someone who has hurt you and whom you have not fully forgiven. Write them a letter in your journal that you do not need to send. Tell them what they did and how it affected you. Then end the letter with the words: I choose to forgive you. This is an exercise for your own heart, not for them.

Quiz Time

Answer these questions in your journal or workbook:

1. What is the difference between forgiveness and reconciliation?

2. According to Colossians 3:13, what is the standard for how we forgive others?

3. What is the point of the parable in Matthew 18:21-35?

4. According to 1 John 1:9, what happens when we confess our sins?

5. Why is refusing to receive God's forgiveness actually a form of unbelief?

This Week's Challenge

Is there someone you need to forgive this week? You do not need to tell them. You do not need to reconcile if it is not safe. But in your own heart, before God, choose to release the debt. Write about what that choice feels like.

New Words to Know

Forgiveness: The choice to release someone from the debt they owe you for hurting you. It is an act of the will, not a feeling.

Reconciliation: The restoration of a broken relationship. It requires both parties and is not always possible.

Unforgiveness: Holding onto a grievance. The Bible warns that it harms the one holding it more than the one it is directed at.

Grace: Receiving what you do not deserve. Forgiveness is an act of grace toward someone who may not deserve it.

Week 46: Serving Others

Why does serving others feel so good even when it is hard?

Zoe's church was organizing a service day. Painting a community center, helping at a food bank, cleaning up a neighborhood park.

She almost did not sign up. She had a lot going on. But something nudged her, and she went.

By the end of the day, she was tired in a way she had not been in a long time. But it was the good kind of tired.

On the drive home, her mom asked how she felt.

'Like I did something that mattered,' Zoe said.

Her mom smiled. 'That feeling is not an accident. You were made for this. Human beings were designed to flourish when they give themselves away. Serving others is not just a nice thing to do. It is how you become most fully yourself.'

We Were Made to Serve

Jesus said in Mark 10:45: The Son of Man did not come to be served, but to serve, and to give his life as a ransom for many.

If the Son of God came to serve, serving is not beneath any of us. It is the shape of the life Jesus modeled.

Galatians 5:13 says: You were called to freedom. But do not use your freedom to indulge yourself; rather, serve one another humbly in love.

Freedom in Christ is not freedom from responsibility. It is freedom to serve without keeping score.

Serving Inside and Outside the Church

Serving happens in two directions.

Inside the church, you use your gifts to build up the body. Teaching, encouraging, giving, leading, hospitality. Every believer has something to contribute.

Not here to be served. Here to serve.

Outside the church, serving is how the gospel becomes visible. Matthew 5:16 says: Let your light shine before others, so that they may see your good works and give glory to your Father in heaven.

When you serve a neighbor, help a stranger, or give to someone in need, you are acting as a representative of Jesus in the world.

Small Acts Matter

Serving does not have to be dramatic to be significant.

Proverbs 19:17 says: Whoever is kind to the poor lends to the Lord, and He will reward them for what they have done.

A meal brought to a sick neighbor. A word of encouragement to someone struggling. Staying after an event to help clean up. These small acts, done faithfully and repeatedly, are the fabric of a serving life.

Key Verses

"The Son of Man did not come to be served, but to serve, and to give his life as a ransom for many." (Mark 10:45)

"Let your light shine before others, that they may see your good deeds and glorify your Father in heaven." (Matthew 5:16)

This Week's Verse to Memorize

Mark 10:45

"The Son of Man did not come to be served, but to serve."

Jesus defined His whole mission as service. Write this verse out and then write one sentence about what it means for your life that the Son of God chose to serve rather than be served.

Activities

Activity 1: Service Inventory

Write down three ways you currently serve others, at home, at school, and at church or in your community. Be honest if any of those categories are empty. Then write one new act of service you could start this week in the emptiest category.

Activity 2: Jesus as Servant

Read John 13:1-17, the account of Jesus washing His disciples' feet. Write down three things that stand out to you about the way Jesus served. Then write one sentence about what His example tells you about the kind of serving God values most.

Quiz Time

Answer these questions in your journal or workbook:

1. According to Mark 10:45, why did Jesus come?

2. What does Galatians 5:13 say we should use our freedom for?

3. What happens when your good works are seen by others, according to Matthew 5:16?

4. Name two places serving happens: inside and outside the church.

5. Why do small acts of service matter?

This Week's Challenge

Do one act of service this week that no one will see or know about. Do it anonymously. Write about how it felt to serve with no possibility of recognition. That kind of serving is closest to the heart of what Jesus modeled.

New Words to Know

Service: Giving your time, energy, or resources to help others without expecting anything in return.

Ransom: The price paid to free someone. Jesus used this word to describe His death: He gave His life to free us.

Stewardship: Managing what belongs to God, including your time and abilities, for His purposes.

Humility: A realistic and honest view of yourself that makes serving others feel natural rather than beneath you.

Week 47: Sharing Your Faith

What do I actually say when someone asks me why I believe?

Daniel had a friend at school who asked him hard questions about his faith.

'How do you know God is real?' his friend asked one day.

Daniel felt nervous. He believed it with everything he had. But he did not know how to explain it.

He talked to his pastor about it.

'I froze,' Daniel said. 'I did not know what to say.'

'That is okay,' his pastor said. 'Sharing your faith is not about having every answer. It is about being willing to say what you know and what Jesus has done for you.'

'What if they ask something I cannot answer?' Daniel said.

'Say you do not know and that you will find out. That is honest. And it shows them that faith is not about pretending. It is about genuine pursuit of truth.'

Sharing Your Faith Is Not Optional

First Peter 3:15 says: Always be prepared to give an answer to everyone who asks you to give the reason for the hope that you have. But do this with gentleness and respect.

Sharing your faith is not the job of professional pastors and missionaries. It is the normal life of every believer.

This does not mean standing on a corner with a megaphone. It means being ready when the conversation comes, and creating space for it to come.

Your Story Is Your Most Powerful Tool

You cannot argue someone into the kingdom. But you can share what you have experienced, and that is hard to argue with.

Your story has three parts. What your life was like before Jesus, or without Him at its center. What happened when you met Him or decided to follow Him. And what is different now.

Sharing faith looks like a conversation, not a performance

That story is yours. No one can take it away or disprove it.

How to Share Well

Listen first. Understand what the other person actually believes and questions before you start talking.

Be honest. If you do not know the answer to a question, say so. Pretending undermines trust.

Point to Jesus, not to your church or your tradition. The person people need to meet is Him.

Pray before and after. You are not responsible for converting anyone. The Holy Spirit does that. Your job is to be faithful and available.

Colossians 4:5-6 says: Be wise toward outsiders; make the most of every opportunity. Let your conversation be full of grace, seasoned with salt.

Key Verses

"Always be prepared to give an answer to everyone who asks you to give the reason for the hope that you have. But do this with gentleness and respect." (1 Peter 3:15)

"Let your conversation be always full of grace, seasoned with salt, so that you may know how to answer everyone." (Colossians 4:6)

This Week's Verse to Memorize

1 Peter 3:15

"Always be prepared to give an answer to everyone who asks you to give the reason for the hope that you have."

Notice that this verse says be prepared, not be perfect. Write it out and then write one sentence about the hope you have and what you would say if someone asked you about it today.

Activities

Activity 1: Write Your Story

Write your personal faith story in three paragraphs. Paragraph one: what was your life or perspective like before you knew Jesus or before He was at the center of your life? Paragraph two: what changed? Paragraph three: what is different now? Keep it honest, personal, and under one page. Practice saying it out loud.

Activity 2: Practice the Conversation

With a parent or trusted adult, practice answering these three questions as if a friend just asked them: How do you know God is real? Why do you believe Jesus rose from the dead? What difference does your faith make in your actual life? After each answer, ask your practice partner what was helpful and what could be clearer.

Quiz Time

Answer these questions in your journal or workbook:

1. According to 1 Peter 3:15, what should every believer be prepared to do?

2. What are the three parts of your personal faith story?

3. Why is your personal story one of the most powerful tools for sharing faith?

4. What should you do if someone asks a question you cannot answer?

5. According to Colossians 4:6, what should your conversation with outsiders be full of?

This Week's Challenge

This week, pray for one specific person who does not yet know Jesus. Ask God to open a door for a conversation. Do not force it. Just be available. Write at the end of the week about whether anything happened, including if nothing did.

New Words to Know

Evangelism: Sharing the good news of Jesus with others who have not yet heard or believed it.

Testimony: Your personal story of faith. What Jesus has done in your life specifically.

Apologetics: Giving reasoned answers for why you believe what you believe. From the Greek word apologia, meaning a defense.

Gentleness and Respect: The manner 1 Peter 3:15 prescribes for sharing faith. The how matters as much as the what.

Week 48: Dealing with Doubt

Is it okay to have doubts about my faith?

Nadia was having a crisis of faith.

She had started reading about science and history, and some of it seemed to contradict what she believed. She felt guilty for having doubts at all.

She told her Sunday school teacher.

'I feel like a bad Christian for even thinking these things,' she said.

Her teacher looked at her steadily. 'Who told you doubt was the opposite of faith?'

'Is it not?' Nadia asked.

'Doubt is not the opposite of faith. Unbelief is. Doubt is what happens when a thinking person takes faith seriously enough to wrestle with it. Almost every great Christian thinker in history had seasons of serious doubt. What matters is not whether you doubt but what you do with it.'

'What should I do with it?' Nadia asked.

'Bring it to God honestly. Dig into it. Ask questions. Faith that has wrestled with doubt and come through the other side is far stronger than faith that has never been tested.'

Doubt Is Not a Sin

Doubting your faith is not the same as losing it.

Thomas doubted the resurrection until he saw Jesus for himself. Jesus did not reject him. He invited him to look more closely. (John 20:27.)

The Psalms are full of honest cries from people who felt abandoned by God. Habakkuk argued with God for an entire book. Job questioned God directly. God honored the honesty of all of them.

Doubt, brought to God honestly, is an act of faith, not a betrayal of it.

What to Do with Doubt

Do not pretend it is not there. Buried doubt does not go away. It festers. Bring it into the open.

Ask the question out loud. Write it down. Find a trustworthy adult to talk it through with.

Dig into it. Many doubts dissolve under examination. If your question has troubled others, people have likely wrestled with it and written about it.

Hold the tension. Not every question has a neat answer. Sometimes faith means trusting God in the space between the question and the answer.

Jude 1:22 says: Be merciful to those who doubt. Extend that mercy to yourself as well.

Faith That Has Been Tested

Romans 5:3-4 says that suffering produces perseverance, character, and hope. The same is true of doubt.

Faith that has never been questioned is fragile. Faith that has wrestled with hard questions and held on is strong.

God is not afraid of your questions. He is big enough for them. Bring them to Him.

Key Verses

"Now Thomas...was not with the disciples when Jesus came. So the other disciples told him, "We have seen the Lord!" But he said to them, "Unless I see the nail marks in his hands...I will not believe."" (John 20:24-25)

"Be merciful to those who doubt." (Jude 1:22)

This Week's Verse to Memorize

Jude 1:22

"Be merciful to those who doubt."

This verse calls us to show mercy to doubters. Write it out and then write one sentence about what it means to extend that same mercy to yourself when you are the one doubting.

Activities

Activity 1: Your Honest Questions

Write down three genuine questions or doubts you have about your faith right now. Be completely honest. No question is too big or too embarrassing. For each one, write one step you could take to begin exploring it: a book to read, a person to ask, a passage to study.

Activity 2: Thomas and You

Read John 20:24-29. Write a paragraph about Thomas: what he doubted, how Jesus responded, and what Thomas said when he finally saw Jesus. Then write one sentence about what Jesus's response to Thomas tells you about how He responds to your own doubts.

Quiz Time

Answer these questions in your journal or workbook:

1. What is the difference between doubt and unbelief?

2. How did Jesus respond to Thomas's doubt?

3. Name two biblical figures who expressed honest doubt or struggle to God.

4. What does Jude 1:22 tell us about how to treat those who doubt?

5. Why is faith that has been tested stronger than faith that has never been questioned?

This Week's Challenge

Write down your biggest doubt or question about faith right now. Then spend fifteen minutes reading or researching one response to it. You do not need to resolve it this week. Just take one step toward it instead of away from it.

New Words to Know

Doubt: Uncertainty or questions about faith. Doubt is not the same as unbelief. It is what happens when a thinking person takes faith seriously.

Unbelief: A settled choice not to trust God or believe His word. This is what the Bible warns against, not honest questioning.

Lament: Bringing pain, confusion, or grief honestly to God. The Psalms model this throughout.

Intellectual Honesty: Being truthful about what you do and do not know or understand. It is a virtue, not a weakness.

Week 49: Suffering and Faith

If God loves me, why do hard things happen?

Lily's family had been through a hard year.

Her dad had lost his job. Her grandmother had passed away. And she had been sick for months with something that was difficult to diagnose.

One night she asked her mom the question she had been afraid to ask.

'If God loves us, why is all of this happening?'

Her mom did not answer right away. She just sat with Lily for a moment.

'I do not know all of it,' she finally said. 'The Bible does not promise that following Jesus means no suffering. In fact, it promises the opposite. But it does promise that God is with us in it, and that He will bring something out of it that we cannot yet see.'

'That is not very satisfying,' Lily said.

'No,' her mom agreed. 'But it is true. And sometimes true is better than satisfying.'

Suffering Is Not a Sign of God's Absence

The Bible never promises that followers of Jesus will be spared from pain. Jesus said in John 16:33: In this world you will have trouble. But take heart! I have overcome the world.

Suffering is not evidence that God is absent or that He does not care. Romans 8:28 says He works all things together for good for those who love Him.

This is not a promise that everything will be comfortable. It is a promise that nothing is wasted.

What Suffering Produces

Romans 5:3-5 says suffering produces perseverance, perseverance character, and character hope.

This requires choosing to trust God while in pain. But the result, a deeper, tested, hope-filled faith, cannot be produced any other way.

First Peter 1:6-7 compares faith tested by suffering to gold refined by fire. The fire does not destroy the gold. It purifies it.

Suffering and the Promise of Restoration

God does not just redeem people. He redeems suffering itself.

Second Corinthians 1:3-4 says God comforts us in all our troubles so that we can comfort those in any trouble with the comfort we ourselves receive from God.

Your pain is not pointless. It is equipping you to help others. And one day, every tear will be wiped away and every wrong will be made right. Romans 8:18 says the suffering of this life is not worth comparing to the glory that will be revealed.

Key Verses

"In this world you will have trouble. But take heart! I have overcome the world." (John 16:33)

"And we know that in all things God works for the good of those who love him, who have been called according to his purpose." (Romans 8:28)

This Week's Verse to Memorize

John 16:33

"In this world you will have trouble. But take heart! I have overcome the world."

Jesus does not promise an easy life. He promises His presence and His victory. Write this verse and then write one sentence about what it means to take heart in the middle of real trouble.

Activities

Activity 1: Where Is God in This?

Think of a hard season in your life, past or present. Write about it honestly: what happened, how it felt, and where you looked for God in it. Then write about whether you can see any ways God was present or working, even if you could not see it at the time.

Activity 2: Romans 8 Study

Read Romans 8:18-30. This is one of the Bible's most powerful passages on suffering and hope. Write down three specific promises Paul makes in this passage. Then write one sentence about which promise means the most to you right now and why.

Quiz Time

Answer these questions in your journal or workbook:

1. What does Jesus promise in John 16:33?

2. What does Romans 8:28 say God does with all things for those who love Him?

3. According to Romans 5:3-5, what does suffering produce?

4. What does 1 Peter 1:6-7 compare tested faith to?

5. According to 2 Corinthians 1:3-4, what is one purpose of the comfort we receive from God?

This Week's Challenge

This week, reach out to someone who is going through a hard time. You do not need to have answers. Just show up. Write about what you said or did and how it felt to offer comfort rather than solutions.

New Words to Know

Theodicy: The theological question of why a good God allows suffering. It is one of the oldest and most important questions in faith.

Perseverance: Continuing to trust and follow God through difficulty without giving up.

Redemption: God turning something broken or painful into something meaningful or beautiful. He redeems people, and He redeems suffering.

Glory: The full, unveiled weight of God's presence and goodness. Romans 8:18 says future glory will make present suffering seem light by comparison.

Week 50: Money, Generosity, and Stewardship

What does God say about money, and why does it matter so much?

Theo's parents sat him down to talk about money.

Not because there was a crisis. But because they wanted him to understand something before he got older.

'Money is not evil,' his dad said. 'But it is powerful, and it can own you if you are not careful.'

'How does it own you?' Theo asked.

'By becoming the thing you trust most. The thing you worry about most. The thing you organize your life around.'

'First Timothy 6:10 does not say money is the root of all evil,' his mom added. 'It says the love of money is. The problem is not what you have. It is what has you.'

Theo thought about that. 'So how do you keep it from having you?'

'Give it away,' his dad said. 'Generosity is the cure for greed. You cannot be tight-fisted and generous at the same time. And every time you give, you remind yourself that the money was never really yours to begin with.'

Everything Belongs to God

Psalm 24:1 says the earth is the Lord's, and everything in it. That includes your money, your possessions, and your abilities.

We are not owners. We are managers. The biblical word is stewards. Everything we have is held in trust for God, to be used according to His purposes.

This changes everything about how you relate to money. If it is not ultimately yours, you can hold it loosely. And holding it loosely is what makes generosity possible.

The Danger of Loving Money

First Timothy 6:10 says the love of money is a root of all kinds of evil. Some people, eager for money, have wandered from the faith.

Money is not evil. But making it your primary source of security, significance, or satisfaction is. Jesus said in Matthew 6:24 that you cannot serve both God and money. They compete for the same place in your heart.

The antidote is not poverty. It is generosity and trust.

The Joy of Generosity

Second Corinthians 9:7 says God loves a cheerful giver. Generosity is not just a duty. It is a joy, when it comes from a heart that trusts God.

Luke 21:1-4 tells the story of a widow who gave two small coins, everything she had. Jesus said she gave more than all the wealthy donors. God measures generosity not by amount but by proportion and heart.

Giving regularly, even small amounts, builds a habit of trust. It trains your heart to say: I believe God will provide. And He always does.

Key Verses

"The earth is the Lord's, and everything in it, the world, and all who live in it." (Psalm 24:1)

"God loves a cheerful giver." (2 Corinthians 9:7)

This Week's Verse to Memorize

2 Corinthians 9:7

"God loves a cheerful giver."

Cheerful giving is the result of a heart that trusts God enough to let go. Write this verse and then write one sentence about what it would look like for you to give cheerfully rather than reluctantly.

Activities

Activity 1: Stewardship Audit

Think about the money you receive, whether from a job, allowance, or gifts. Write down what you currently do with it: spending, saving, giving. Then write what percentage goes to each. Is your giving intentional or occasional? Write one change you could make to become a more intentional steward.

Activity 2: The Widow's Offering

Read Luke 21:1-4. Write a paragraph about what Jesus noticed, what He said, and what it tells us about how God measures generosity. Then write one honest sentence about what kind of giver you currently are and what kind you want to become.

Quiz Time

Answer these questions in your journal or workbook:

1. According to Psalm 24:1, who owns everything?

2. What is the difference between being an owner and being a steward?

3. What does 1 Timothy 6:10 say is the root of all kinds of evil?

4. Why did Jesus say you cannot serve both God and money?

5. How did Jesus measure the widow's generosity in Luke 21:1-4?

This Week's Challenge

Give something away this week that costs you something. Not a leftover. Something you actually wanted or valued. Write about what it felt like before and after. Generosity that does not cost you anything is not yet generosity.

New Words to Know

Stewardship: Managing something that belongs to someone else. All we have belongs to God; we are His stewards.

Generosity: Giving freely and joyfully, beyond what is required or expected.

Tithe: The practice of giving a tenth of your income to God. It is rooted in the Old Testament but the principle of proportional giving carries through the New Testament.

Contentment: Being satisfied with what you have. First Timothy 6:6 says godliness with contentment is great gain.

Week 51: Rest, Sabbath, and Margin

Why did God command rest, and what does that tell us about how we should live?

Rosa's schedule was packed.

School, sports, homework, church, family commitments. She was busy from the moment she woke up until she fell asleep.

One Saturday her dad cancelled everything.

'We are doing nothing today,' he said.

Rosa felt guilty at first. She had things to do. But by afternoon, something had relaxed inside her that she had not even known was tense.

'Why does this feel so good?' she asked her dad.

'Because you were made for it,' he said. 'God built rest into the rhythm of creation. It is not a reward for finishing everything. It is a gift given at the beginning. The Sabbath was made for people. Not the other way around.'

'But there is always more to do,' Rosa said.

'There always will be,' her dad said. 'That is why rest is a discipline, not a reward.'

God Rested, and So Should We

Genesis 2:2-3 says God rested on the seventh day and made it holy. This is not because He was tired. It is because He was modeling a rhythm for His creation.

Exodus 20:8-10 makes Sabbath one of the Ten Commandments. God takes rest seriously enough to command it.

Mark 2:27 records Jesus saying the Sabbath was made for people, not people for the Sabbath. Rest is a gift, not a burden. But it requires intention. It will not happen on its own.

What Rest Is For

Rest is not laziness. It is the deliberate act of stopping in order to remember who is really in charge.

When we rest, we are saying: the world will not fall apart if I stop. God is holding it together, not me.

Rest restores. Consistently skipping rest is not productivity. It is a slow drain on every area of your life.

Psalm 23:2-3 says God leads us beside quiet waters and restores our soul. He does not drive us to exhaustion. He leads us to restoration.

Margin and the Unhurried Life

Margin is the space between your capacity and your commitments. Without margin, there is no room for the unexpected, for people, or for God.

Jesus regularly withdrew to lonely places to pray. (Luke 5:16.) If He needed time apart, we certainly do.

Building margin is countercultural. Everyone around you will be busy. But a life with no margin has no room for what matters most. Guard your rest. It is not wasted time. It is investment in everything else.

Key Verses

"Remember the Sabbath day by keeping it holy." (Exodus 20:8)

"The Sabbath was made for man, not man for the Sabbath." (Mark 2:27)

This Week's Verse to Memorize

Mark 2:27

"The Sabbath was made for man, not man for the Sabbath."

Rest is a gift, not a burden. Write this verse and then write one sentence about what it means that God designed rest for your benefit, not as an obligation to fulfill.

Activities

Activity 1: Schedule Audit

Write out your typical weekly schedule. Count how many hours you have committed to activities, homework, screens, and social time. Then count how many hours are unscheduled. Write one sentence about whether your schedule has any real margin in it. If not, write one thing you could reduce or remove to create space.

Activity 2: A Day of Rest

Plan and take one partial or full day of rest this week. No homework if possible. No screens unless necessary. Do something restoring: a walk, reading for pleasure, time with family, creative play. Write at the end about what you noticed. What was hard? What was good? What did rest reveal that busyness had been hiding?

Quiz Time

Answer these questions in your journal or workbook:

1. What does Genesis 2:2-3 say God did on the seventh day and why?

2. What does Jesus say in Mark 2:27 about the purpose of the Sabbath?

3. What does rest tell us about our relationship with God?

4. What is margin, and why does it matter?

5. According to Psalm 23:2-3, what does God lead us to?

This Week's Challenge

Build one regular rest habit into your life this week that you can keep. Not a vacation day, but a simple daily or weekly practice: a quiet morning before checking your phone, a tech-free evening, a walk without earbuds. Write about what you chose and what you want it to become.

New Words to Know

Sabbath: A day of rest commanded by God in Exodus 20. The word means to stop or cease. It is about stopping work, not just being less busy.

Margin: The space between your capacity and your commitments. A life without margin has no room for God, people, or unexpected needs.

Rest: Not laziness, but the deliberate and trusting act of stopping in order to restore and remember who is in charge.

Rhythm: A regular pattern of activity and rest. God built rhythm into creation from the beginning.

Week 52: A Life of Faith: Putting It All Together

After everything you have learned this year, what do you do with it now?

It was the last day of the year.

The youth group had gathered for a final session. Their leader stood at the front with a simple question.

'What has changed in you this year?'

The room was quiet at first. Then one by one, students began to speak.

One said she finally understood why Jesus had to die.

Another said he had started praying for the first time, really praying, not just saying words.

One said she used to think faith was for weak people. She did not anymore.

Their leader smiled. 'You have covered a lot of ground this year. But I want you to hear something clearly. You have not just learned about God. If what you have studied has done its work, you have come to know Him. And knowing Him changes everything. It changes who you are, how you live, what you hope for, and who you love. That is what a life of faith looks like. Not perfect. But pointed in the right direction. And held by the One who never lets go.'

You Have Been Learning the Shape of the Faith

Over fifty-two weeks, you have covered the foundations of Christian belief.

Who God is. The Trinity. Scripture. Creation. Sin. Salvation. The Holy Spirit. Prayer and worship. The church. Angels and spiritual warfare. The end times. And now, how to live it all out.

None of this was just information. Theology is not the study of ideas about God. It is the study of God Himself. And the goal was never just to know more. It was to know Him more.

Faith Is a Journey, Not a Destination

You have not arrived. Neither has anyone else.

Philippians 3:12-14 says Paul himself had not yet arrived. But he was pressing on, reaching forward, moving toward the goal. That is the posture of a life of faith. Not perfect, but pressing on.

Some days will be clear and full of God's nearness. Other days will be dry and difficult. Both are normal. Both are part of the journey.

Hebrews 12:1-2 says: Run with perseverance the race marked out for you, fixing your eyes on Jesus, the pioneer and perfecter of faith.

The Invitation That Never Closes

Everything you have learned points to one thing: God wants to be known by you.

He made you for that. He sent Jesus for that. He gave you His Spirit for that. He gave you the Bible for that. He gave you the church for that.

The invitation is open. It has always been open. It will always be open.

John 10:10 says Jesus came so that you may have life, and have it to the full. That life is available to you. Right now. In every ordinary moment of every ordinary day.

This is not the end of the journey. It is the beginning of living what you now know.

Key Verses

"I press on toward the goal to win the prize for which God has called me heavenward in Christ Jesus." (Philippians 3:14)

"Let us run with perseverance the race marked out for us, fixing our eyes on Jesus, the pioneer and perfecter of faith." (Hebrews 12:1-2)

This Week's Verse to Memorize

Hebrews 12:1-2

"Let us run with perseverance the race marked out for us, fixing our eyes on Jesus, the pioneer and perfecter of faith."

This is the picture of a whole life of faith: a race, run with perseverance, with eyes fixed on Jesus. Write this verse out slowly. Then write one sentence about what it means to fix your eyes on Jesus specifically in your life right now.

Activities

Activity 1: Your Theology in Your Own Words

Without looking back at your notes, write one paragraph each about: who God is, what the gospel is, and how you want to live in light of what you know. Use your own words. Be honest about what you still have questions about. This is a snapshot of where you are right now in your faith. Keep it. Come back to it in a year.

Activity 2: A Letter to Your Future Self

Write a letter to yourself to be read in one year. Tell your future self what you learned this year, what changed, what you are still wrestling with, and what you want to remember. Seal it and ask a parent to keep it somewhere you will not open it until the date you write on the front.

Quiz Time

Answer these questions in your journal or workbook:

1. What is the difference between knowing about God and knowing God?

2. According to Philippians 3:12-14, did even Paul feel like he had arrived spiritually?

3. What does Hebrews 12:1-2 say we should fix our eyes on?

4. What does John 10:10 say Jesus came to give us?

5. Name three things you learned this year that have most changed how you think about God or faith.

This Week's Challenge

This week, do something to celebrate what God has done in you this year. Share something you have learned with someone who did not go through this workbook. Teach it to a younger sibling. Write it in a letter. Tell a friend. What you give away, you keep.

New Words to Know

Theology: The study of God. Not just ideas about Him, but the pursuit of knowing Him as He has revealed Himself.

Perseverance: Continuing faithfully over the long term. Hebrews 12 uses the image of a long-distance race.

Pioneer and Perfecter: The title Hebrews 12:2 gives to Jesus. He blazed the trail of faith and brings it to completion.

Abundant Life: Jesus's phrase in John 10:10. Not a life free of difficulty, but a life full of God's presence, purpose, and love.

You Finished the Journey

Congratulations! If you reached the end of this book, you and your child have taken an incredible journey together. You explored who God is, discovered important Bible truths, and talked about how faith shapes everyday life.

Teaching children about God is one of the most meaningful investments a parent, teacher, or mentor can make. The time you spent reading, discussing, and learning together will continue to shape their faith for years to come.

Thank you for allowing this book to be part of that journey.

Before you go, could we ask you for one small favor?

Reviews help other parents, homeschool families, and ministry leaders discover resources that help children understand Christian beliefs in a clear and engaging way.

If this book helped your child learn about God, the Bible, and faith, would you take a moment to leave a short review?

It does not have to be long. Even a few words can help other families decide if this book is right for them.

You might mention:

- What your child enjoyed most
- What surprised you about the lessons
- How the weekly format worked for your family
- Whether the activities or quizzes helped learning

To leave a review, simply scan the QR code below or visit the link.

https://www.amazon.com/review/create-review/?ie=UTF8&channel=glance-detail&asin=1969357053

Thank you again for choosing this book and for investing in your child's faith. Your encouragement, conversations, and example will make a lasting difference.

With gratitude,

Wonder & Word Press

Helping children understand who God is, what the Bible teaches, and how to live out their faith every day.

Answer Key

Your Free Answer Key Is Right Here

Wondering if you got it right? Want to go back and review what you learned? Scan the QR code or click on the link to download the complete Answer Key for all 52 weeks. It's totally free.

Inside you will find answers to every quiz question from every chapter, organized by unit and alphabetically, so they are easy to find. Whether you are checking your work, studying for fun, or going back through a unit with a parent or teacher, it is all right there waiting for you.

https://bit.ly/404chbm

Thanks for spending this year getting to know God. He has been worth every question.

Theology Dictionary

Every week in this workbook, you encountered words that theologians, pastors, and serious Bible students have used for centuries. Words like incarnation, justification, sanctification, and eschatology. They are not just vocabulary. They are keys that unlock deeper understanding of who God is and what He has done.

We have collected every one of those words into two free dictionaries, just for you.

Scan the code or click on the link for the **Alphabetical Theology Dictionary**, where all 171 words are arranged from A to Z. Perfect for looking something up quickly or exploring on your own. https://bit.ly/TheologyDictionary_Alphabetized

Scan or click on the link for the **By-Week Theology Dictionary**, where the same words are organized by the week they appear in this book. Perfect for studying alongside each chapter as you go. https://bit.ly/TheologyDictionarybyWeeks

Every definition includes a pronunciation guide so you will always know how to say the word out loud, and each one is written to actually make sense, not just to sound impressive.

Scan. Save. Start learning.

Resources

Bavinck, H. (2019). *The wonderful works of God: Instruction in the Christian religion according to the Reformed confession*. Lexham Press.

Berkhof, L. (1996). *Systematic theology* (Combined ed.). Wm. B. Eerdmans Publishing.

DeYoung, K. (2018). *The biggest story Bible storybook*. Crossway.

Frame, J. M. (2013). *Systematic theology: An introduction to Christian belief*. P&R Publishing.

Grudem, W. (2020). *Systematic theology: An introduction to biblical doctrine* (2nd ed.). Zondervan Academic.

Horton, M. (2011). *The Christian faith: A systematic theology for pilgrims on the way*. Zondervan.

Packer, J. I. (1993). *Knowing God*. InterVarsity Press.

Ryrie, C. C. (1999). *Basic theology: A popular systematic guide to understanding biblical truth*. Moody Publishers.

Sproul, R. C. (2015). *Everyone's a theologian: An introduction to systematic theology*. Reformation Trust Publishing.

Starr Meade, S. (2011). *Training hearts, teaching minds: Family devotions based on the shorter catechism*. P&R Publishing.

The Holy Bible, English Standard Version. (2016). Crossway.

The Holy Bible, King James Version. (1769/2017). Cambridge University Press.

The Holy Bible, New International Version. (2011). Zondervan.

Ware, B. A. (2019). *Big truths for young hearts: Teaching and learning the greatness of God*. Crossway.

www.ingramcontent.com/pod-product-compliance
Lightning Source LLC
LaVergne TN
LVHW081404110826
845149LV00010B/1657